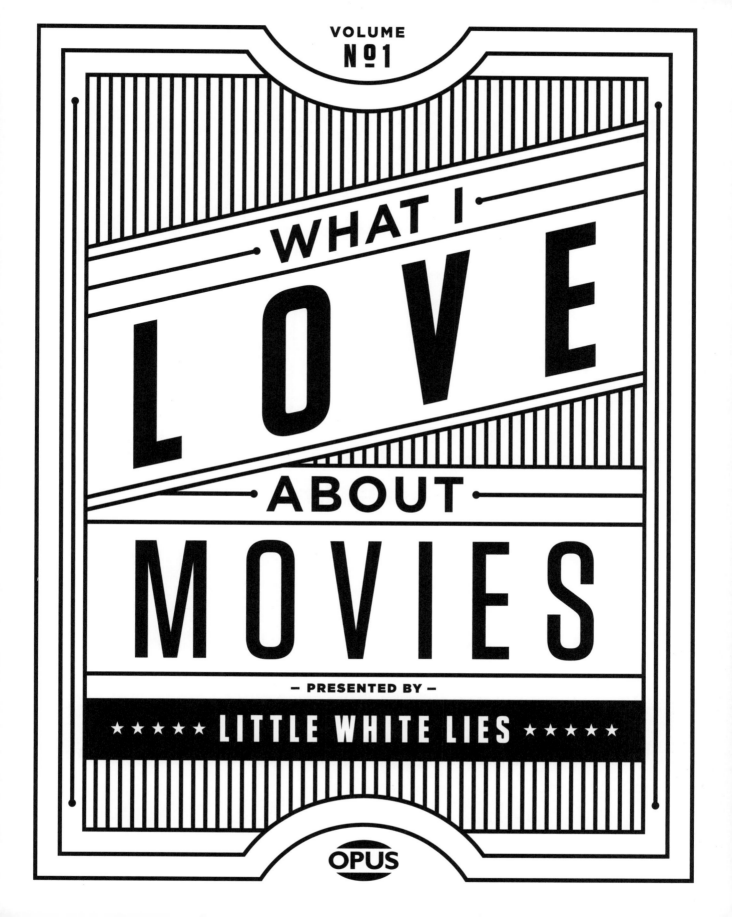

WHAT I LOVE ABOUT MOVIES
by David Jenkins, Adam Woodward; creative direction by Timba Smits

Cover artwork by Mario Zucca

First published in the United States by OPUS in 2014
by arrangement with Faber & Faber Limited, London

ISBN: 978-1-62316-062-3

ISBN: 978-1-62316-062-3 (print); 978-1-62316-063-0 (kindle); 978-1-62316-064-7 (epub);
978-1-62316-065-4 (Adobe PDF)

FIRST EDITION
10 9 8 7 6 5 4 3 2 1

A Division of Subtext Inc., A Glenn Young Company
44 Tower Hill Loop • Tuxedo Park, NY 10987
Publicity: E-mail OPUSBOOKSPR@aol.com
Rights enquiries: E-mail GY@opusbookpublishers.com
All other enquiries: www.opusbookpublishers.com

OPUS is distributed to the trade by The Hal Leonard Publishing Group
Toll Free Sales: 800-524-4425
www.halleonard.com

EDITOR
DAVID JENKINS
david@tcolondon.com

DEPUTY EDITOR
ADAM WOODWARD
adam@tcolondon.com

CREATIVE DIRECTOR
TIMBA SMITS
timba@tcolondon.com

DESIGNER
OLIVER STAFFORD
oliver@tcolondon.com

PROJECT MANAGER
TARYN PATERSON
taryn@tcolondon.com

STAFF WRITER
SOPHIE MONKS KAUFMAN
sophie@tcolondon.com

ACCOUNT DIRECTOR
BINDI KAUFMANN
bindi@tcolondon.com

MEDIA SALES EXECUTIVE
GEORGE JENNINGS
george@tcolondon.com

PUBLISHER
VINCE MEDEIROS
vince@tcolondon.com

GENERAL MANAGER
WENDY KLERCK
wendy@tcolondon.com

THIS BOOK IS DEDICATED TO
PHILIP SEYMOUR HOFFMAN
1967–2014

"It's like you come onto this planet with a crayon box. Now, you may get the eight pack, you may get the 16 pack, but it's all in what you do with the crayons – the colours – that you're given. Don't worry about colouring within the lines or colouring outside the lines. I say colour outside the lines, you know what I mean? Colour all over the page; don't box me in! We're in motion to the ocean. We are not land locked! I'll tell ya that... So, where do you want out?"

From the film

WAKING LIFE BY **RICHARD LINKLATER** (2001)

CONTENTS

WHAT I LOVE ABOUT MOVIES

AN INTRODUCTION

WORDS BY DAVID JENKINS

It usually begins with silence. Anything between a few seconds and half a minute. Occasionally, even more than that. Then, most often, an arm is raised and employed as a makeshift chin rest. The forefinger might oscillate in a light stroking movement on the lower jowl. The eyes dart sideways. There's always a deep sigh, sometimes pensive, sometimes annoyed, mostly pensive and annoyed. The wait is excruciating, exacerbated by a verbal false-start or a preliminary untangling of words and ideas. A clock ticks. What will happen next? And then, suddenly...

This is, generally speaking, the instantaneous physiological reaction displayed by movie folk when *Little White Lies* poses the question, "What do you love about movies?". I can tell you firsthand, it is not a wholly pleasant experience. The unspoken rule is that this question is left until the end of the interview, to form a bracing intellectual digestif, if you will. It caps things off nicely, but would also prove tough to come back from if dropped into the middle of a conversation about a specific movie, project or scene. It's tough to gauge whether people actually like to be asked this question. There's no obvious frame of reference, so they are forced to think and react and be articulate under great pressure. When the words arrive and they're good and insightful and passionate and funny, the feeling of relief cannot be beaten. As replicated in this volume, we've opted to retain an exact transcription of the responses we've collected over the years, as it really gives a sense of these people who are removed from us but somehow part of our everyday life as a palpable physical presence.

So why do we burden ourselves with such a high-risk conceptual sign-off? In truth, no-one really knows. It has become part of *Little White Lies* lore, an ancient rite which now just comes as a knee-jerk reaction. Perhaps the question was born out of a natural affirmative streak; the idea that the function of *Little White Lies* is a conduit for movie passion, each issue a shrine to an artwork that we simply want our readers to get excited about and then go and enjoy for themselves.

It's hard for us to fathom the ramifications of this question, as we are essentially asking these people, why did you dedicate your life to the creation of transitory entertainments which drift through the public consciousness like so many scattered autumn leaves? There's also the assumption that these people do, in fact, love movies. They might despise movies for all we know. This might be considered a menial day job to pay the bills and secure a rosy financial future for any/all offspring. Indeed, some have directly expressed their ire at what they see as a creative rot within the modern industry, where cookie-cutter action movies cascade from a production line to be forgotten almost instantly.

Yet the question transcends the notion of whether you like movies or you don't like movies. It's calling into question a specific definition of movies, how they function on some deep personal and societal level, what they mean, what they represent, and even what they are. Thinking, for a moment, what you love about movies forces you to break them down to their molecular fundamentals and concoct a personalised set of terms and conditions into which you must frame your answer. All credit is due to the subjects of this book who have managed to formulate a set of responses which suggest they don't just make movies, but they understand them too.

What's good for the goose and all that, so now as an experiment I will attempt to ask myself this question. It's not quite the same, as there's no clock ticking or spotlight shining on me.

SO, WHAT DO I LOVE ABOUT MOVIES?

[*Long awkward pause*] Well, thank you for asking... As I am not on the spot and don't have a PR person attempting to usher me from the room as my allotted interview time has come to an end, I will take this moment to actually ponder my response deeply which, I must admit, is something that I have never done before. In the spirt of the diverse and detailed array of answers delivered by our august roster of subjects, I'll attempt to make my response personal but hopefully with a ring of relatable, universal truth.

I have decided that my answer will encompass a trio of short, possibly tall tales which roughly detail my cinematic upbringing as well as painting a series of non-religious but most definitely spiritual epiphanies which duly augmented my adoration and understanding of the film medium. These vignettes will be individually named and catalogued in chronological order. So, onwards...

PART ONE:
THE HORROR MOVIE

My father is what you might term a "film buff," though he would probably never refer to himself as such. Prior to my birth, he spent much of his leisure time driving around London in a (no doubt) clapped-out vehicle trying to catch as many rep screenings as he could physically fit into a day. He spent a lot of time at the Electric Cinema in Notting Hill, London, a venue where the central character in Olivier Assayas' sublime *Something in the Air* sees the light in the film's climactic scene. There was even a family rumour that my parents' "plans" for their wedding night were scuppered when it transpired that *Quatermass and the Pit* was playing on television.

My earliest memory of being profoundly emotionally affected by a film occurred late one night when I was about four or five years old. My mother had gone to bed and my father had remained downstairs to watch a movie. My childhood home was – to adopt estate agent parlance – "cosy," and added to the fact that my bedroom door was made of a wood that seemed to have next-to-no soundproofing qualities, I was awoken by the televisual melee emanating from down below. I began to quietly descend the stairs. My father saw me and coaxed me to join him.

I entered the living room and began to watch the television. The images I saw are, to this day, seared in to my mind. I have never been able to forget them. They plagued my dreams for years to come. Here's a description: the film was in colour, from the '50s or '60s and either sci-fi or a horror. A young man and woman enter a room together. They are dressed in futuristic uniforms and both sport a chilling rictus grin. The camera pans back to reveal two operating tables placed side-by-side. The pair remove their garments – I think skimpy futuro-underclothing remained, but I can't recall for certain. Still smiling, they both lay down on the tables. A few beats of silence. There may have been some dialogue. Then suddenly, a series of holes open up in the wall. Creepy-crawlies of all sizes and colours stream out in giant clumps. They cover the floor, and then soon begin to climb up onto the operating tables. The man and woman just lie there, contented, not moving a muscle. They are then covered head to toe in ants and spiders and grubs and slugs and beetles and centipedes. At the point where their entire bodies were completely obscured, the memory fades. I either blacked out, decided this wasn't for me, or my father realised that I might be a little young for this crazy jazz.

My father has no recollection of this night or the title of the film he was watching at the time. I have since described the footage I saw to many a learned film scholar, though no-one has ever been able to correctly place it. Yet, I know that if I ever saw the footage again, I would recognise it instantly. So to round off part one, what I love about movies is their capacity for what you might call surprise nostalgia. One day, just when I least expect it, I'll see this film again, and while it may mean absolutely nothing to everyone else in the room, it will, for me, be loaded with fuzzy existential import. I remain scared and excited for that day to arrive.

PART TWO:
THE BOGUS JOURNEY

To return to my father, it was not long before he was using my brother and I as bargaining chips to go to see more movies. His insistence on carting us from the suburbs of London to Leicester Square, so that we might experience these films in what he termed a "proper" cinema, was admirable. Yet it quickly got to the point where we wanted to see certain films that were beyond his prestige purview. The 1991 film *Bill and Ted's Bogus Journey*, by director Peter Hewitt, was one such title we insisted upon viewing, yet it was deemed by my father as unworthy of the long trip into town, so our local fleapit, The Enfield Canon (which later became the Enfield ABC and then later still became Tesco) would have to suffice.

There's not much more to this story than to say that both myself and my brother left the cinema breathless, overwhelmed and overjoyed. It was, we agreed in a rare détente, the best film we'd ever seen and, by extension, ever made. My father remained ominously silent. We got into the car, enthusing about our favourite moments – the scene in which the evil Bill and Ted peel back their skin to reveal their robot innards was definitely mooted. Then, my brother timidly asked my father, "What did you think, Dad?". The response was instant and unmerciful: "Total crap." We both burst into tears.

As traumatising as that was, in hindsight it taught me a crucial lesson about the nature of movie appreciation. Loving or loathing a movie does not predicate the necessity of a consensus. Diversity of taste and nuance of expression (however curt) should be championed wherever possible. A war of words is entirely healthy, as long as matters don't spill over into street brawls. Movies provoke expression and passion. I love movies, but I also love the people who love movies. And, most of the time, I love the ways in which they say they love those movies. Does that make sense?

PART THREE:
THE CAROUSEL

Flash forward to the here and now. My undisputed favourite film of all time is Jacques Tati's 1969 opus, *Play Time*. I saw it for the first time in 2008 and have watched it at least once a year since. I was working on the film desk at *Time Out London* at the time, and I only decided to watch it because my then-colleague, the mightily bearded Tom Huddleston, referred to it as one of the most dull movies he'd ever been forced to sit through. Our tastes differed somewhat, so I thought what the hell. The film sees Tati's beloved Monsieur Hulot loping happily, gracelessly around a glass-and-steel rendering of a hypothetical Paris that's been enveloped by the scourge of modernism. There's barely a narrative to speak of, and the action plays out over a single day. It's more akin to a free-form urban ballet, where the precise choreography of human movement creates a kind of theatrically heightened riff on reality. During my first watch, I'll admit that I didn't really get it. It's a film which I now understand requires gradual adjustment to its fanciful and radical rhythms.

It comes across as a series of sketches, and Hulot himself is not so much the star of the film as he is the comedic nucleus around which the large majority of the film's antic humour orbits. I'll admit that my appreciation stems more from the unfathomable delicacy of its craft than its success as a film comedy. I probably laughed louder and longer at the *Jackass* movie, if I'm being honest. Yet it's a film I can watch over-and-over and appreciate anew each time.

During its climactic flurry, Tati orchestrates a scene in which a nose-to-tail traffic jam fills out an entire roundabout and is visually and sonically re-contextualised as a funfair carousel. I find it very hard to not watch the final 15 minutes of *Play Time* without bursting into floods of tears. Nothing conventionally sad happens, per se. And I'm not weeping at any undue melodrama which has seeped into the storyline. For a long time I had no idea why the waterworks came on at this exact point every time. But I recently worked it out. I'll try and articulate it in the best way I can. It moves me that a human being would deign to think in those terms. That someone could have that idea, process it, and then execute it. It's so silly and so throwaway, and yet it's an utterly uncynical visualisation of an idea that could never be expressed via any other mode of communication. Even though I wouldn't say I adored all of his movies, I view Tati as cinema's great genius. *Play Time* for me is perfection, and exists as a glorious, incomprehensible gesture that could only be articulated via celluloid. Movies are a way of looking at the world. They're a tool for understanding it. I suppose I love that movies can make you cry without you knowing exactly where the tears are coming from.

So that's my answer.

What's yours?

KEY TO BIOGRAPHIES:

DJ I David Jenkins

AW I Adam Woodward

SMK I Sophie Monks Kaufman

VR I Vadim Rizov

WHAT I LOVE ABOUT MOVIES

· FEATURING ·

FRANCIS FORD COPPOLA

"It is just the most diverse and complete art form that I know of — that uses everything: uses music, uses emotion, uses image, uses writing and structure. I often think that there's only been a hundred years of cinema and yet the amount of masterpieces that have been done are amazing. I can only conclude that the human race was waiting for cinema so they could pour this out because how else could there have been so many great films even in the first 30 years? So it's sort of a divine collection of all of human aspiration and art forms. I often think, 'What kind of movies would Goethe have made?' Because he was both scientist and poet and theatre person. Or other people in the past."

▼

We might forget it now, but Francis Ford Coppola remains the godhead of '70s cinema, its unalloyed sense of creativity as much as its embodiment of financial excess. The French New Wave redefined the artisans of classic-era Hollywood as film artists, the camera standing in as a pen or paintbrush. By the '70s, directors like Coppola were conscious of that tag and of their status as artists, and the pictures they produced were the result of the total autonomy which they were granted. But this power was earned, from hardscrabble labour and an ascent through the clammy ranks. Coppola earned his spurs, like so many of his contemporaries, in the world of B-movies, collaborating with Blaxploitation godhead Jack Hill on the cheapjack sex comedy, *Tonight For Sure* (1962).

Like Martin Scorsese and Joe Dante, he too was soon taken under the wing of schlock producer Roger Corman and was given the reigns of the low-budget horror quickie, *Dementia 13* (1963), his first non "nudie" picture. Coppola got the gig due to the fact that he had worked in the sound department of another Corman feature, *The Young Racers* (1963), which had come in under budget. Of course, even though young Coppola was gaining a handle on the technical particulars of the business, it would be nearly a decade until he truly announced himself to the world with *The Godfather* (1972), followed by the unimpeachable triple-header of *The Godfather 2* (1974), *The Conversation* (1974) and *Apocalypse Now* (1979). The bubble spectacularly burst in 1982 with *One From The Heart*, his underrated love letter to the artificial allure of Las Vegas nightlife. It was to become a folly too far, and Coppola has claimed that all films made between 1983's *The Outsiders* and 1997's *The Rainmaker* were done to clear his debts.

By suppressing the supple grandeur of his formative years, Coppola injected a Corman-like rawness to films such as despair-laced youth movie, *Rumble Fish* (1983) and, more recently, in angular monochrome melodrama, *Youth Without Youth* (2007) and his Val Newton-inspired horror curio, *Twitx* (2011). Coppola is hardly the filmmaking giant he once was, but his fervent commitment to personal ideals and belief that film is foremost an artist's medium mean his work is still met with a measure of wonderment and intrigue. **DJ**

WHAT I LOVE ABOUT MOVIES

• FEATURING •

CLAIRE DENIS

"It's... an instant. A fraction of time in any film where suddenly there is a gap – maybe an ellipse or a cut? – that leads me into the movie. I never enter through a shot. I need a cut. I need an ellipse. I need a gap. And then... it's... something. It's an experience that I cannot define or compare to anything else. Even the beauty of a shot, for me it's not enough. It's not enough! A shot exists. But it's the cut. It's the cut. The cut does it. A cut is always a gap, even if it's very, very small. It's where you can... enter."

Illustration by

MISS LED

Claire Denis' camera alternately jolts and glides smoothly over human flesh in screen-filling close-ups, defamiliarising skin into lunar landscapes. She's less about plot, more about attention to how everyday corporeal properties can hypnotise us — most often, bodies moving through a grainy, often tangible celluloid fug charged with sex and danger. The two aren't automatically intertwined: in 2002's *Friday Night*, Denis announced herself as one of the few directors capable of rendering non-romantically-charged passion without descending into a moral or physical apocalypse. It's the constant potential for danger that makes the momentary pleasure of safe release all the sweeter. A languid night can slip into quiet violence or euphoric connection with no indication which way things are trending. Sex, rewarding and dangerous as it can be, is what adults and teenagers have when they're not dancing: the continuum from one to the other is similarly slippery.

Colonial Africa, where Denis was brought up until age 14, is the site of her 1988 debut *Chocolat*, terrain revisited more apocalyptically 21 years later with *White Material*. At "home" — rarely the cuddly familiar Paris of the stereotypical "French film," but its dimmer alleyways or outlying suburbs — Denis stands with the immigrants and children of ex-colonial subjects making a go of it: she's matter-of-factly multicultural.

Despite her penchant for casting from the same loose ensemble, she cannot be confined within a recycled circle of motifs. Eros, certainly, saturates everything, dangerously or innocuously – this idea formed the basis for her languid 1999 film, *Beau Travail*. There's also an hilarious moment in 1996's *Nenette and Boni* where a frustrated pizza maker sublimates his frustration into kneading dough, finding polymorphous perversity in innocent flour. The same antennae, picking up on similar and sometimes deeply buried sexual signals, can make observed environments warmly rejuvenating (2008's *35 Shots Of Rum*; *Friday Night*; the 1994 TV film, *US Go Home*) or more ambivalently charged: 2001's *Trouble Every Day* is a nightmare conflation of seemingly straightforward sexual appetite and seductively destructive addiction. A tonal manic-depressive, Denis' disinterest in straightforward narration can give way to the thorny convolutions of 2004's *The Intruder*, 2009's *White Material* or 2013's *Bastards*: implicitly and explicitly violent movies, worrying themselves into potentially unparsable narratives, circling around traumatic elisions too horrific to view head-on. **VR**

ADMIT ONE
ONLY

WHAT I LOVE ABOUT MOVIES

• FEATURING •

JAKE GYLLENHAAL

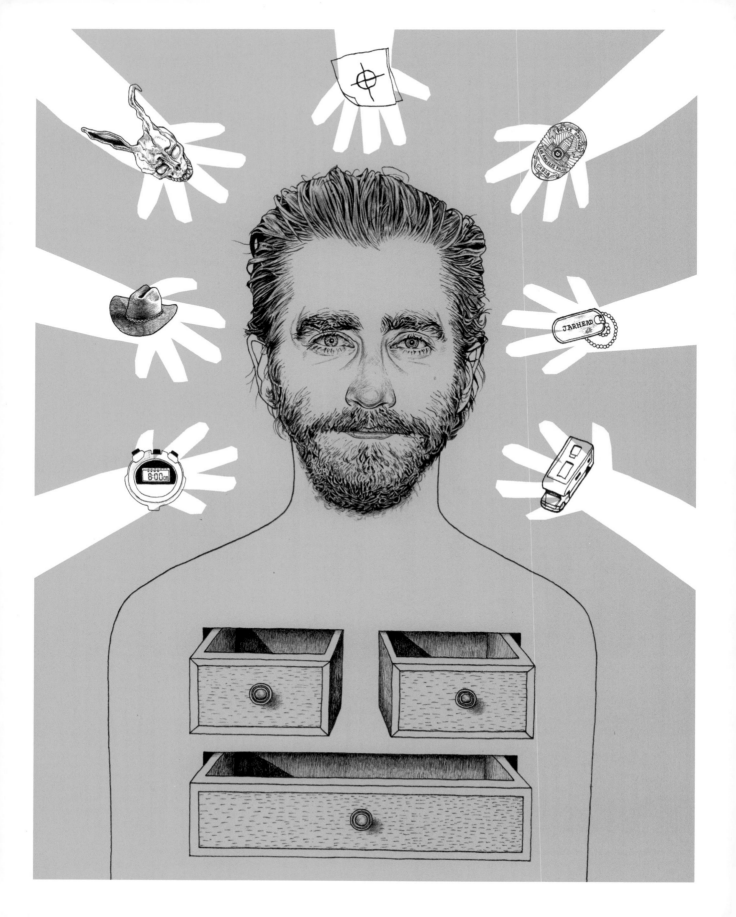

"Two things, if I have to keep it short... I love the brilliance and the vast verisimilitude – is that the right word? – of minds that come together to tell a story, to make a movie. The people, unlike any other business in the world, even the experts from other fields who just come in for a day... it's unreal. It's bordering on unreal. The access that is granted into these other worlds, to see what really happens, no other business gets that. Even journalists! It's true! They don't get that type of access and that type of perspective on the world. To me, that's what I love about making movies. What I love about movies? Movies are the closest things we have to dreams. They're a reflection of, at the highest level, at the best place, they're a reflection of who we are as a culture, and who we are individually at a certain period of time."

Illustration by

ADAM CRUFT

Whether he's playing a disturbed teenager (2001's *Donnie Darko*), a jaded GI (2005's *Jarhead*) or an obsessive cartoonist-turned-investigative reporter (2007's *Zodiac*), there's something reassuringly familiar about watching Jake Gyllenhaal at work. Perhaps it's the winning mix of quiet intensity and boy-next-door likeability he frequently projects? Maybe it's his emotive, trusting eyes? Somehow, Gyllenhaal has always felt like one of the good guys. It's no wonder he's often cast as unlikely heroes and honourable lawmen — albeit typically with some kind of debilitating cross to bear. Roles in *Prisoners* (2013) and found-footage cop drama *End of Watch* (2012) proved Gyllenhaal can play tough with the best of them, but there's a tenderness and a fragility to him that's instantly engaging. Think back. Has there ever been a Gyllenhaal character you didn't end up rooting for in some small way?

Gyllenhaal was weaned on cinema from a young age — his father was a director and his mother a screenwriter — and, by the time he landed his debut lead in 1999's *October Sky* at 18 years of age, he had already made three feature appearances, a figure which would be significantly higher were it not for the protective influence of his parents. In 2005, Ang Lee's *Brokeback Mountain* provided Gyllenhaal with more mainstream exposure, his Academy Award-nominated supporting performance signalling his arrival on Hollywood's biggest stage. Since then, Gyllenhaal has been on a hot streak that shows no sign of cooling off.

What's most surprising about this is that Gyllenhaal is, by his own admission, extremely picky about parts. The quantity and quality of Gyllenhaal's output over the best part of the last decade shows he has a keen eye for both a tight script and a director on the rise. His two films with Québécois writer/director Denis Villeneuve, *Prisoners* and *Enemy*, both shot in 2013, underlined his reputation for playing fundamentally good guys who come perilously close to stepping off the path of righteousness. And yet, having successfully made the transition from child actor to cult favourite to top-billed leading man, Gyllenhaal is comfortably smart and talented enough to transcend lazy charges of typecasting. **AW**

ADMIT ONE
ONLY

WHAT I LOVE ABOUT MOVIES

• FEATURING •

PEDRO ALMODÓVAR

▼

"When I started talking about films, and when I started to watch films myself, I remember feeling that the less real life there was in a film – the less real it seemed – the far better for us. When I was young and I used to go to the cinema, all the films back then were from Hollywood, and I think the more unreal the film was, the more we loved it. At the end of the day, film for us was just a great escape; for an hour-and-a-half you could just sit down and forget about your own life and live a parallel life in a parallel world completely different from your own."

Illustration by
ALEC DOHERTY

The Spanish director Pedro Almodóvar acted in a small but vital role for his licentious, post-punk 1980 feature debut, *Pepi, Luci, Bom and Other Girls on the Heap*. During a raucous party scene, male attendants assemble for a game of "Erecciones generales" (General Erections) for which Almodóvar, playing emcee, proceeds to measure the length and width of the participants' unmentionables. This sly, roistering brand of burlesque was emblematic of La Movida Madrileña, a wave of enlightened, countercultural rebellion ushered into Spanish society following the fall of Franco and the gradual softening of state censorship.

While this kitsch sense of humour can be detected across the entire length and width of Almodóvar's astonishing directorial back catalogue, his career can be divided into two distinct phases which are cleanly split by his 1999 film, *All About My Mother*. On a superficial level, 1999 was the point where Almodóvar attained broad mainstream acceptance, widespread critical plaudits and even a clutch of major industry awards. The film also signals a pointed maturation in both style and his mode thematic inquiry; the Cukor-esque, high-camp capering of films like *Women On The Verge of a Nervous Breakdown* (1988) or the bald sexual provocations of *Matador* (1986) were suppressed rather than expunged, as Almodóvar embraced and expertly riffed on classical sources like the seditious melodrama of Douglas Sirk (2009's *Broken Embraces*, 2006's *Volver*) and the gender-based body horror of Georges Franju (2011's *The Skin I Live In*).

Almodóvar's attraction towards strong female lead characters lends cohesion to these two phases as well as making a strong case for him being one of the great male directors of women alongside Kenji Mizoguchi and Rainer Werner Fassbinder. Ex-cabaret singer and the grande dame of Spanish cinema, Carmen Maura, remained his star and muse for all of his films up to 1990's *Tie Me Up, Tie Me Down*, where he began a collaboration with diminutive sexpot, Victoria Abril. By the time of 1997's noir-infused Ruth Rendell adaptation, *Live Flesh*, he began perhaps his most popular and creatively fecund partnership with Penelope Cruz, an actor who went on to deliver a career-best performance in 2006's *Volver*. **DJ**

ADMIT ONE

ONLY

WHAT I LOVE ABOUT MOVIES

FEATURING

RICHARD AYOADE

"A lot of the things that I love about movies are quite hard to talk about. It can make it sound like you don't love that thing, but the things I love are so private in a way, it's almost embarrassing to reveal, or it almost feels glib or flip to say. I don't know... a film that you really like can make you feel completely differently about things after it than you did before. You see things in a way that would not have been possible were it not for that film. A very specific thing that I think film does differently is that you can register a change in thought in a face contemporaneously with other people's ability to take in that information. It actually allows you a level of objectivity and subjectivity that is almost instantaneous. When it happens it's thrilling. I think *Persona* is one of those films... there's a scene where Bibi Andersson hides some glass and is waiting for Liv Ullmann's character to step on it... and that is a brilliant example of the subjectivity of seeing it through Bibi Andersson's eyes and also being able to feel for Liv Ullmann and see it unfold. It's such a... So much is happening, and you're watching it, but you're having thoughts that are different to just the series of images. And that's... yeah, perhaps not a quote for the poster..."

Illustration by

OIVIND HOVLAND

▼

The late, great Japanese director Nagisa Oshima, responsible for such movie classics as *In the Realm of the Senses* (1976) and *Cruel Story of Youth* (1960), was known locally as much for his TV wrestling punditry as his work in cinema. The same might be said of London-born filmmaker and actor Richard Ayoade. He too divides his time between making idiosyncratic, off-kilter movies and appearing on light entertainment panel shows. A professed worshiper at the crooked altar of Ingmar Bergman (*Persona* is his favourite movie), Ayoade cuts something of a strange figure on the British film landscape, and his ardent cinephelia almost seems at odds with the type of films expected to be made on UK soil.

His lauded 2010 debut feature, *Submarine*, appeared more indebted to the fun-time likes of Richard Lester or the hyper-colour stylistics of Nicolas Roeg than social-realist godheads like Mike Leigh and Ken Loach. Set in Wales and based on the debut novel by Joe Dunthorne, the film offered a veritable sugar-rush of formal invention while confirming Ayoade's keen eye for the ironic composition. A harbinger for *Submarine* was the bold and brilliant TV sitcom *Garth Marenghi's Darkplace* from 2004, which Ayoade co-wrote and directed alongside the lead, Matthew Holness. A sharp satire on pompous horror fiction and low budget '80s genre television, *Darkplace* saw Ayoade perfectly reproduce (and lovingly mock) the cack-handed visual tropes of the era.

With only two feature films under his belt, it's probably unwise at this point to unpick Ayoade's auteurist DNA, particularly as 2013's *The Double* is so totally different in subject and tone to his celebrated debut. An awkward romance is all that remains as Ayoade ventures into a Gilliam-inspired steampunk/clockwork hinterland and monitors the scuppered attempts of Jesse Eisenberg's nebbish office drone to woo copy girl Mia Wasikowska when his exact double clocks on for a shift. What really stands out from *The Double* is Ayoade's diverse palette of reference points, from the smart-mouthed office politics of Billy Wilder's *The Apartment* (1960) and the numerous stylistic/musical hat-tips to Jean-Luc Godard, to the ultimate division and conversion of souls seen in his beloved *Persona.* **DJ**

ADMIT ONE
ONLY

WHAT I LOVE ABOUT MOVIES

FEATURING

QUENTIN TARANTINO

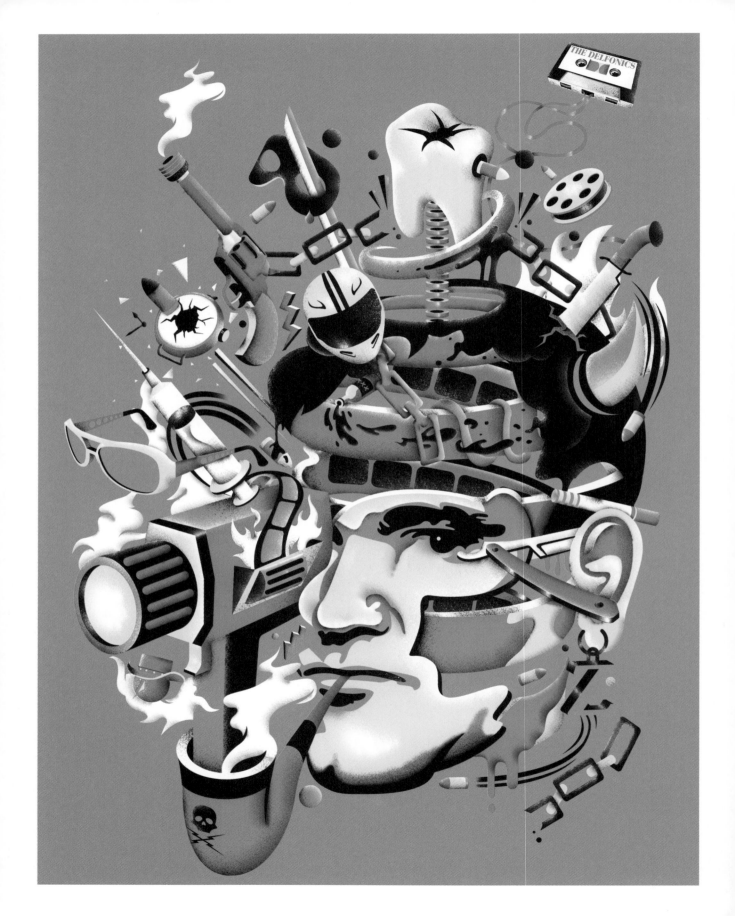

"Huh. Haha... Well, um... Okay, yeah. So, the thing is, you ask me that question, over the course of my life, it'd probably be different answers. That's what's interesting, I guess. I think maybe eight years ago, I might have said the storytelling aspect of it. But now, it's the artform. It would be the artform itself. When I kind of enjoy movies the most now, is when I get that voracious aspect of going through a career or a genre or a country's cinema. This grand film study that goes on my whole life."

Illustration by

I LOVE DUST

The big, bad survivor (and then some) of the '90s American independent film boom, Quentin Tarantino was the man who famously assigned his success as a filmmaker not to the conformo-factory of film school, but to the arduous process of actually watching lots of films. As the mythos goes, QT spent his formative years divided between staff work at a VHS rental shop and hunkered down on the balding seats of his local fleapit. As a writer, his films are characterised by the fine art of digression and the acknowledgement that, in reality, human dialogue is seldom at the wholesale service of some contrived dramatic arc. Yet films like *Reservoir Dogs* (1992) and *Pulp Fiction* (1994) offered few if any concessions to bland social realism, instead creating a heightened form of reality peppered with obscure, self-conscious cultural references. The cadence and delivery of dialogue was as vital as character or storyline.

His later works consist of cut-and-dried revenge narratives that have been artfully (and sometimes garishly) festooned with postmodern trinkets and baubles which, in turn, lend gravitas, humour and subtextual richness to potentially hackneyed material. 2009's *Inglourious Basterds*, for instance, charted the violent fortunes of a cadre of Jewish soldiers and self-styled Nazi hunters ("This is the face of Jewish vengeance!") as they attempt to sabotage a gala screening of a German propaganda film. The ironic hue of the drama and the knowingly gaudy characterisations shrouded provocative intimations on the nature of revenge fantasies and the dangerous power of cinema to make them "real". He pulled off a similar trick with American slavery via 2012's *Django Unchained*.

Prior to that, Tarantino's films had taken a turn for the academic (except for 1997's soulful career outlier, *Jackie Brown*, adapted from Elmore Leonard's novel, *Rum Punch*) that pushed his rampant cinephila to the fore. This phase resulted in some of his greatest works, including the colourful *Kill Bill* diptych and his quasi-experimental paean to the grindhouse sub-genre, *Death Proof* (2007). In that film, Kurt Russell essays a murderous stunt driver named Stuntman Mike who, when about to move in for a series of violent kills, glances directly at the camera and offers a wry smile. This is QT's project in a nutshell. **DJ**

ADMIT ONE
ONLY

WHAT I LOVE ABOUT MOVIES

FEATURING

KELLY REICHARDT

▼

"Wow, big question! Let me see... Well, I grew up in Miami in the '70s, which was sort of a cultural black hole. I got very into photography around sixth grade and I wanted to travel around the world taking pictures, but then I moved up to Boston and there was all this activity that really blew my mind. I was 18 at that point and I was seeing so many things that I'd never seen before. So it was then that I realised I wanted a film camera not a photo camera. It's that discovery which I love and which has stuck with me, every time I see a kid shooting their first piece of film or kids that have grown up with video. Being able to make something with a bunch of other people that you like is a pretty good feeling."

Illustration by

MONTSE BERNAL

The flame of 1970s American independent cinema remains alight and glowing brightly in the hands of Portland-based director and film scholar, Kelly Reichardt. And yet her films also proffer an insidious sense of doom and existential dread, as the apparent simplicity of the stories she tells (mostly based on the writings of Oregonian author, Jon Raymond) acts as a fable-like façade for matters more complex and politically substantive. Take her celebrated second feature, *Old Joy* (2006), which has itself taken on life as an industry shorthand for a brand of (often lesser) bucolic, loose-weave, realist drama which prides mumbled but honest intimacy over contrived plot machinations and the crutch of genre.

It's the tale of two salty old pals who take a drive into the woodlands on the outskirts of Portland in order to indulge in the manly ritual of bathing in a hot spring. The awkward patter shared by these long-estranged and now very different men delivers the film's superficial pleasures, but also provides a sense of lilting melancholy as well as posing philosophical questions about class rifts, the difference between town and city and a sense of societal breakdown when it comes to the simple act of human communication.

While her debut, *River Of Grass*, from 1994, felt like a more traditional, indie-flavoured road movie, it offered clear signs of great things to come. Instead of scaling-up after the success of *Old Joy*, Reichardt wound things down further with 2008's masterful smalltown fairytale, *Wendy and Lucy*. The theme of intrepid Americans ceaselessly searching for something they've lost in a land they don't know as well as they think continued in *Meek's Cutoff* (2010). This anachronistic range western, shot in boxy Academy ratio and delivered from the perspective of its harried female characters, possessed a simple moral conceit which harked back to classics of the genre such as William Wellman's *The Ox-Bow Incident* (1943) and John Ford's *The Searchers* (1956). Again working with Raymond, Reichardt produced what appeared to be her most directly political work in *Night Moves* (2013), a coolly calibrated Melvillian crime caper involving a gang of young eco-terrorists which slowly transforms into a disquieting essay on the nature of causality. **DJ**

ADMIT ONE
ONLY

WHAT I LOVE ABOUT MOVIES

• FEATURING •

JOHN HURT

"There are many things I love about movies. I like the language. You don't often get the full opportunity of speaking that language. Language is, of course, the wrong word, as it immediately makes you think of literature. It's the opposite of literature. It's concerned with images on a screen. That's the mode of information. Cinema is not a story with pictures. It is the moving image which is the story. It's what you can do with that "language", for want of a better word. "Format"? That's not the right word either. It's another form of communication. And I love that form. The directors I think of immediately that you absolutely can't mistake are people like David Lynch... There are many directors you'd call "literate". Stephen Frears is literate. But he has a terrific understanding of images on screen and the power of using shots to say what he wants to say without getting into the purple passages of literature. You remember the images."

Illustration by

RUPERT SMISSEN

Not only will John Hurt go down as one of Britain's greatest film and television actors, but also as one of the world's greatest screen narrators. His voice, as full-bodied and mellow as a vintage claret, has the uncanny ability to imbue any and all visuals with an air of high gravitas and easy authority. And yet, there's something grounded and cordial about it too; he is both all-seeing God and skilled pub raconteur. His narration makes a movie. Take the fairytale-like commentary overlaying Lars Von Trier's *Dogville* (2003); his spry intonation fostered an atmosphere of paranoia and unease, reminding us of the film's quaint, storybook sensibility and pointed unreality while forcing us to endure all manner of physical horrors. Atom Egoyan took advantage of Hurt's husky tones and their ability to hold the attention for a 2000 adaptation of Samuel Beckett's *Krapp's Last Tape*, in which an old man listens to a recording of himself from 38 years previous.

Hurt's extraordinary and diverse 50-years-and-counting career is impossible to pigeonhole, though there is a noticeable break between his early and late screen roles. During the '70s and '80s, he gravitated towards the tragic naif – good men forced to endure immense suffering. An early highlight was his wide-eyed illiterate patsy in Richard Fleischer's grubby kitchen-sink horror film, *10 Rillington Place*, from 1971. His Kane is introduced as the empowered and affable executive officer of the mining ship Nostromo in Ridley Scott's *Alien* (1979), only to later be dispatched in one of cinema's most operatically gruesome and nightmarish sequences. In 1980, Hurt's astounding take on the hobbling Victorian circus freak John Merrick in David Lynch's *The Elephant Man* proved he was an actor able to channel pure empathy and pain through thick layers of a latex mask.

During his later years, Hurt has developed into the role of the puckish elder sage who commands respect from his many acolytes. He played Garrick Ollivander, the world's foremost maker of wands, in *Harry Potter and the Deathly Hallows: Part 1* (2010). An affiliation with American director Jim Jarmusch extended from 1995's quixotic neo-western *Dead Man*, through to his doddering turn as a vampiric Christopher Marlowe in 2013's *Only Lovers Left Alive*. Turns in movies like Guillermo del Toro's *Hellboy* (2004) or Bong Joon-ho's *Snowpiercer* (2013) present him as a link to the past, a bedraggled fount of knowledge and wisdom who must be allowed to spill his guts before it's too late. **DJ**

WHAT I LOVE ABOUT MOVIES

· FEATURING ·

SIMON PEGG

"Sitting in the dark with a bunch of people you don't know; there's a wonderful community feeling about that. I worry about things like 3D and the new frame-rate issue. There's something to be said for film on film in the cinema. It's being diminished, I think."

Illustration by

MISS LOTION

▼

Many British readers of this volume will have likely grown up alongside London-born writer and actor Simon Pegg. He's the very definition of the kind of bloke you'd want to go down the pub with (his official website is named "Peggster"), and he styles himself as such. He's spoken of now as paid-up member of the Hollywood cognoscenti, a headline star and perma-trudger of red carpets who has lent his redoubtable comic talents to such behemoth franchises as JJ Abrams' *Star Trek* movies and the fourth *Mission: Impossible* title. It has, though, taken years of hard graft to reach this point, as he originally made a name for himself as a comedy bit player in such superior UK TV sketch shows as *Big Train* (1998–2002). If there was a biographical blueprint for the Pegg persona, then the two cherished series of the sitcom *Spaced* (1999-2001).

Spaced was the first platform to zero in specifically on Pegg's adeptness as a writer and satirist, as well as an actor able to bundle a fuzzy pathos with a character whose prime function was to generate laughs. It also consolidated his relationship with director Edgar Wright, who shared his screwball, postmodern vision of urban life, and the actor Nick Frost, soon to become a de facto screen partner. Yet unlike the conventional DNA of classic screen pairings, the Pegg/Frost dynamic transcends the need for standardised characterisation. During the three films that make-up the so-called "Three Flavours Cornetto trilogy, " (2004's *Shaun of the Dead*, 2007's *Hot Fuzz* and 2013's *The World's End*), the dramatic relationship between the two actors is in a constant state of flux. In *Shaun*, Pegg was highly strung and Frost was laid-back. In *The World's End*, the roles were completely reversed. They've even been cast as absolute equals, when they voiced the roles of the Thompson and Thomson in Steven Spielberg's digitally-animated *The Adventures of Tintin* (2011). His greatest performance to date was care of Wright's *The World's End*, in which he expertly channeled a combustible mix of tragic frailty and manic energy into a quasi-deranged middle-aged alcoholic, attempting to complete the regional pub crawl he once heroically failed as teenager. **DJ**

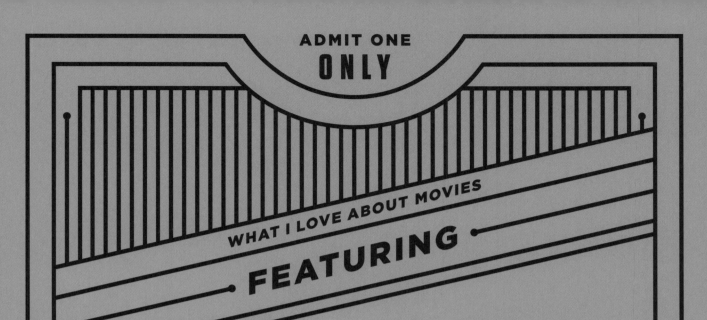

ADMIT ONE
ONLY

WHAT I LOVE ABOUT MOVIES

FEATURING

MILA KUNIS

"It's escapism for an hour-and-a-half. That's what I love about movies. I think that whether you're happy or sad, for an hour-and-a-half you're in a completely different world."

Illustration by

BEC WINNEL

Bumbling radio personality and nervy 25-year-old Chris Stark got the interview of his life in 2013, just as actress Mila Kunis cemented her reputation as something of a dream girl. During the seven-minute interview slot intended for the standard-issue promotion of wizard prequel, *Oz the Great and Powerful*, Kunis encouraged digressions into the details of Stark's social life, apparently sharing his enthusiasm for Watford Football Club and the ingredients of alcoholic tipple, the 'LAD-bomb'. Her staunch good humour and earnest delight at no longer having to repeat the same PR-stamped lines ensured that the video went viral and anchored a fantasy to reality. A beautiful Hollywood starlet had entertained the thought of hanging in a grotty UK boozer with a bunch of braying goons.

It's little wonder that the actress who has voiced Meg Griffin since the 1999 launch of Seth MacFarlane's surreal animation serial, *Family Guy*, has a lively sense of fun. She stayed loyal to MacFarlane, taking a girlfriend role as he graduated to filmmaking with bad taste bromance, *Ted* (2012). Watching Kunis glittering opposite two aggressive slobs gave new life to the term "pearls before swine".

Her most prominent and celebrated 'serious' role has been as Lily, the maddening and seductive ballet dancer opposite Natalie Portman in Darren Aronofsky's *Black Swan* (2010). Both actresses endured punishing schedules of dancing and exercise, a commitment Kunis seemed to relish despite the torn ligament and dislocated shoulder it ended up costing her. The Wachowski siblings' 2014 sci-fi epic, *Jupiter Ascending*, once again demanded serious physical training. But it's a necessary evil, particularly for Kunis's first lead in a motion picture.

Kunis still has everything to play for. Will the rambunctious, comedic side of her character be allowed to shine in a role that is also serious, or will her marketable looks and physical dedication escort her through a career of functional but soulless hackwork? Whatever the answer to this hypothetical quandary, there's no denying her remarkable screen presence, nor the fact that, in a world dominated by male screen comics, Kunis is very much leading the revolution. **SMK**

ADMIT ONE
ONLY

WHAT I LOVE ABOUT MOVIES

FEATURING

OLIVIER ASSAYAS

"It's, you know, of course very difficult to answer but it's difficult for everybody to answer. I suppose I love a lot about movies – it's what my life is about. I think that the chance you have to give life, to give body and flesh to characters you have imagined, or to see come to life in front of your eyes things that you have imagined, dreams or fantasies – and getting paid for it... There is something that has to do with art, something that has to do with magic, and which has, I suppose, a metaphysical dimension. Movies have to do with the very thin bond between realities and dreams, between fact and imagination, between what you are and what you could be, between reality and how you transcend it. And ultimately all those lines end up blurring. In film after film, movies take you to pretty weird places and it's something you can share with an audience. Movies occupy a unique place in our world."

Illustration by

KAROLIN SCHNOOR

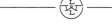
Aged 13 in May '68, young Olivier Assayas needed a satisfactory outlet to reconcile his anti-Stalinist leftism with a sense of having been born too late to join in the last period of productive political ferment. For him, making a movie channels everyone's talents into one momentarily productive Situationist site, a safe creative sphere in a stultifying world. Paradoxically, his first masterpiece, *Irma Vep* (1996), depicts the opposite: a film set being torn apart by every conceivable level of administrative dysfunction. An ageing, over-his-head auteur finds himself unable to cope with the demands of modern filmmaking, a scenario conceived by a writer/director whose background as a *Cahiers Du Cinema* journalist meant he was savvy about film's steady mutation into a global entity on sometimes irreconcilable cultural and business levels.

A keen student of globalisation and its discontents, Assayas' typically twitchy camera is ever on the literal move. In *Irma Vep's* globe-trotting spiritual successor *demonlover* (2002), shots of negotiations for the rights to anime porn and torture broadcasts are refracted through translucent and reflective surfaces, necessitating constant visual reorientation. The corporate buyers become the bought in the unnerving ending, tortured as part of programmes they thought they could control.

Assayas worries about precisely nameable forces — corporate, political, economic — whose global operation can't be stopped by any amount of cogent diagnosis or counteracting goodwill. In 2010's three-part *Carlos*, the eponymous assassin goes from '70s terrorist-as-revolutionary to post-Cold War assassin-hack-for-hire, chewed up by the same global regimes he helped bring to power. Satellite countries caught in the shadowboxing Cold War struggle between capitalism and communism struggle to carve out their own destiny, and not even a violent freelancer can achieve a small degree of independent autonomy.

The same struggle of displacement can take place on a more modest scale: 2008's *Summer Hours* is a stereotypically "French" chamber drama about the reunion of a family whose members sprawl from China to New York. Juliette Binoche's character announces that the family house means nothing to her, much like France itself. Home is a thought framework, not a physical site, and movies become a momentary but vital base to reflect and regroup. **VR**

ADMIT ONE
ONLY

WHAT I LOVE ABOUT MOVIES

FEATURING

JUDE
LAW

"That's a good question... The escape. I was hooked by the cinema at a very, very young age. It doesn't really matter what's going on outside or what time of day it is, what kind of life point you're at, you can slip into this darkened room and lose yourself and be taken places. It triggers the imagination which I think is the most powerful thing we have."

Illustration by
MARIO ZUCCA

For some actors, good looks are a good joke, smoothing their passage through complicated plots but otherwise to be worn lightly. George Clooney and Matt Damon fall into this category, but Jude Law could never be a blithe fellow member of Danny Ocean's posse. In his Hollywood debut *Gattaca* (1997), Law plays a bitter ex-swimmer with perfect genetics who is rendered irrelevant by an accident that left him a paraplegic. His looks are golden, but with mobility restricted and prospects null, he seethes with ineffectual self-loathing, a template for Law's oft-prickly screen persona.

Off-screen, Law is comfortable cashing in on his looks as the longtime face of Dior perfume. On-screen, he'll occasionally condescend to play handsome and happy, though he's rarely been less convincing than as an innocuously charming leading man in the dire romance *The Holiday* (2006). His comfort zone is centred on a physical challenge or handicap, preferably one diminishing his looks: lousy teeth and yellow fingernails in *Contagion* (2011) and *Road To Perdition* (2002), a receding hairline in *Anna Karenina* (2012).

Deformation can be a matter of internal character as much as looks. In 2004's *I Heart Huckabees* (another definitive part), Law is advertising man Brad Stand, whose success as an advertising executive is as fragile as his American accent. An encounter with rogue psychiatrists simultaneously unmoors his sense of commercial achievement, marriage and self-esteem as he freefalls into frantic gibbering. Just looking like a success doesn't enable him to inhabit the part for long before panic takes over. Not for nought did he inherit Michael Caine's first signature role in a 2004 remake of *Alfie*, another character for whom easy success doesn't come at all easy.

In Steven Soderbergh's *Contagion*, Law is a loathsome online journalist whose disdain for fact-checking is as dangerous as the pandemic he's distorting; in the same director's *Side Effects* (2013), he's actually right about everything but his sweaty paranoiac appearance undermines his quest to find sympathetic listeners. The ultimate Law part may be as robot Gigolo Joe in Steven Spielberg's *A.I. Artificial Intelligence* (2001): with the smooth skin and unnatural plastic shine of a mannequin, he's a soulless specimen whose looks are more creepy than enticing. **VR**

ADMIT ONE
ONLY

WHAT I LOVE ABOUT MOVIES

• FEATURING •

SPIKE JONZE

"When I think about it, it's creativity that inspires me. When somebody makes something that I can get lost in. You know, when it sort of captures my imagination. And I just think about the feeling I had when I saw Maurice Sendak's books and, you know, there's a sequence where the little kid falls through the floor and through the ceiling of the next floor... And then he falls out of his pyjamas and he lands in the big thing of dough. Like when I first saw Michel Gondry's music videos. I'd started directing videos and I kept seeing videos with his name on them. And after a few of them, I said, 'Who is this guy?' There was just magic there, like the Björk 'Human Behaviour' video or the Rolling Stones video or the Massive Attack video. The same with Chris Cunningham when I saw his videos. Just anything that feels like, you know... Like somebody's just... That is just... Making something that I can just fall into. You're just consumed with it."

Illustration by
CHRIS DELORENZO

A mong the teeming egos of Hollywood, it is unusual to find a man so humble and so closely wedded to his creative output that it's impossible to make out where the work ends and he begins. The films of Spike Jonze (born Adam Spiegel) and, by extension, his character, continue to evolve. First he made skate videos, then he cut characterful storylines for such musical royalty as the Chemical Brothers, the Beastie Boys, Björk and Arcade Fire.

Back then, his name was synonymous with that of screenwriter Charlie Kaufman. He wielded the camera while the wild-haired Kaufman penned the pirouetting dialogue for *Adaptation* (2002) and *Being John Malkovich* (1999). It took until 2013 for the first film entirely written and directed by Jonze to arrive. *Her* marked his first solo mission as writer and director and is endlessly thought-provoking on topics of love, gender, relationships, technology and the future. It is also a work that feels fully a part of him and – excitingly – a part of us too.

Theodore Twombly (played by Joaquin Phoenix) is a lonely writer nursing heartbreak in a tangerine-hued future city. Theodore's self-awareness is articulated through dialogue that would be considered too on-the-nose if only it weren't so intelligent and wistfully funny. Jonze's writing feels like the confession of a man who can only express himself through the coalescence of artistic urges. Though smaller in ambition, his 30-minute 2010 short *I'm Here*, in which Andrew Garfield voices a love-struck robot, possesses the same intimate tone.

The future, as a setting, provides a handy blank slate for his ability to work with a cool, clean aesthetic, abetted by an affecting soundtrack from regular collaborators Arcade Fire. *Her* is a story of love and artificial intelligence drenched in love and real intelligence. The formula sounds simple, but shares with its creator a life of wisdom and heartache behind it; the film needs every drop of this heady fuel to work. Personal alchemy is what lends vivid sensitivity to Jonze's characters and their predicaments. It is the secret ingredient that makes him and his work now, more than ever, a flattering mirror to our romantic selves. **SMK**

ADMIT ONE
ONLY

WHAT I LOVE ABOUT MOVIES

FEATURING

HELEN MIRREN

———

"I think I love the privacy of the experience of watching a movie. When I watch a film it's just me and the screen, and I love that; the intimacy of that."

———

Illustration by
GRACE HELMER

Helen Mirren came of age in a world where her patina of coiled eroticism made her the subject of a leering, jeering type of attention. Even the venerated king of the UK chat-show circuit, Michael Parkinson, let his objectivity slide on a broadcast in 1975 asking whether her "equipment" got in the way of being taken seriously. Mirren's response was to play up elements of a sex kitten persona, letting a strap fall on her dress to expose a bare shoulder, even as she purred out challenges to Parkinson's sexist assumptions. This teasing, gently-mocking side of her character has lingered down the years, enabled by the sure knowledge that she possesses the depth and seriousness once thought to be unfathomable in an attractive, assertive woman.

While a more bashful actress might have attempted to dull her sensual edges, Mirren did the reverse, opting for challenging roles such as the abused wife and secret lover in Peter Greenaway's beautiful monstrosity, *The Cook, The Thief, His Wife and Her Lover*, from 1989. Degradation, nudity and individualism defined her femme fatale-ish character. The same could be said of her small but vital role as a sultry gangster moll in John Mackenzie's 1980 Brit classic, *The Long Good Friday*. Even when bounding to Oscar glory playing HRH Elizabeth II in Stephen Frears' 2006 almost-biopic, *The Queen*, she managed to bring a subversive edge to this primped, pampered and emotionally cloistered monarch.

The Royal Shakespeare Company is where her dramatic sensibilities were honed and grounded, and Mirren made her mark in a slew of classic stage roles, forming an attachment to the theatre that has never been severed. Work is regular and varied and the sense is that Mirren, whose friends include over-erudite rebel comic, Russell Brand, is able to enjoy a world that has finally caught up with her sophistication. **SMK**

ADMIT ONE
ONLY

WHAT I LOVE ABOUT MOVIES

• FEATURING •

JIA ZHANGKE

▼

"To be honest, movies weren't really my first love. In my youth, there were two other main pathways for expressing myself – writing novels and creating art. I went to university to study art. It was only at university that I really connected with movies. I went to a screening of Chen Kaige's *Yellow Earth,* and it completely changed what I thought about the medium. There was hardly any speaking in that film, just these amazing shots and images strung together in this gorgeous manner. It really moved me. And it helped me realise the potential that movies can have on life. With film, you don't need to do a lot to touch people."

Illustration by

MOOSE & YETI

Jia Zhangke's trajectory from scrappy underground filmmaker to state-approved director demonstrates the full (i.e. extremely limited) range of career opportunities available to Chinese directors. Being "underground" means shooting without permission but not necessarily courting arrest, a strategy Jia employed for his first three features *Pickpocket* (1997), *Platform* (2000) and *Unknown Pleasures* (2002). Those works proved him an instant master of the long-take static shot that dominated late '90s and early millennial arthouse cinema. It's a style sometimes reflexively denounced as appealing solely to privileged film festival viewers, but Jia's adeptness with an admittedly rarefied idiom is far from exclusive, giving many not-particularly-political global viewers an incentive to witness what the state-administered, top-down transition from a command economy to quasi-fettered capitalism looks like.

When Jia became a state-sanctioned filmmaker with 2004's *The World*, his lack of overt condemnation made it possible for him to fictionalise the listless lives of unmotivated theme-park workers in a transitional economy. To follow, he systematically recorded the construction of China's Three Gorges Dam and its attendant displacement of 1.5 million people in *Still Life* (2006), *Dong* (2006) and *Useless* (2007), movies that repeatedly return to images of entire villages smashed and destroyed to make room for the new body of water. One is a narrative, another a documentary, the third a hybrid, but, like Werner Herzog, Jia casually embeds verité within staged scenes and vice versa.

Transitioning from the riverside to the city, *24 City* (2008) and *I Wish I Knew* (2010) considered the dismantling of old industrial architecture and the sprawl of new high-rise construction. It's a change that's simultaneously concrete and unfathomably swift; no wonder that in *Still Life*, a new building reveals itself as a literal UFO, blasting from its base and into space. With 2013's *A Touch Of Sin*, Jia took on his riskiest gambit politically, dramatising four documented incidents of endemic violence across China. Approved in its script phase yet reportedly never shown domestically, it's another uneasy blend of non-professionals and actors, fictional scenario and documentary footage, a tricky meld in which near-empirical records of China's changing terrain and Jia's unapologetically subjective filtration of recent national history became inseparable. **VR**

ADMIT ONE
ONLY

WHAT I LOVE ABOUT MOVIES

FEATURING

MICHEL GONDRY

"Ummm... Well, there is the time I watched movies before I started to make them. I like them because they're a nice, strong distraction. It's a medium that's been around for over 100 years and is still evolving, so that's interesting also. You can watch a movie then talk about a movie – they take me away and there's this magical moment where I enter into a sort of dream state. I dream a lot and I'm very curious about my dreams. It's not that I always try to explain them, sometimes it's obvious why you dream about a certain subject. Movies, for me, share many of the principles of dreams. They can be painful a lot of the time, but often there is the occasional sweet moment too. I tend to write about my dreams. When I wake up, I write a sentence or a little paragraph. Since I became a director, I've actually started to direct my own dreams. I put myself in situations of high drama. I interact with my dreams. I can see myself co-ordinating the action. I had a dream last night where I was reading a newspaper and the image on the front cover was animated. And then I told my brother about it. I've never dreamed about this before."

Illustration by
ELIOT WYATT

There's a puckish artisanal eccentricity which binds the creative output (not just feature films, but also music promos, art installations, internet videos and TV shows) of French filmmaker Michel Gondry. He's as interested in the artistic capacity of sticky tape and used toilet rolls as he is advances in digital technology or the sensuality of camera movement. His charmingly rambling documentary profile of linguist and philosopher Noam Chomsky, *Is The Man Who Is Tall Happy?* (2013), took two years to produce, as Gondry decided to personally animate the film with a hand-cranked 16mm Bolex camera. Much like his stylistic partner-in-crime, Spike Jonze, Gondry was given a career leg-up when collaborating with writer Charlie Kaufman. 2004's *Eternal Sunshine of the Spotless Mind* was a whimsical, star-studded romantic science-fiction fable which pondered the elasticity and malleability of the mind with breathtaking assurance and wit.

The question of what goes on inside our heads is something that has fascinated Gondry since the early days of his career, and he uses filmmaking as an exploratory tool to probe and prognosticate the metaphysical links between mental and cinematic imagery. 2006's *The Science of Sleep* was his most literal evocation of this project, a film which fluidly slipped between the streets of contemporary Paris and a fantastical, hand-moulded dream world. Similarly, 2008's *Be Kind, Rewind* offered a sweetly nostalgic and amusingly post-modern ode to cinema's glorious tactile qualities, its function as a community rallying point and its magical potential as an ad-hoc creative outlet. This bald celebration of community could also be seen in his documentary, *Dave Chappelle's Block Party*, in which the American stand-up comedian and sketch comic plays emcee for a laid-back concert on the streets of Brooklyn, New York.

Perhaps even more so than feature films, Gondry is a master of short-form filmmaking, a format that comfortably houses his ostentatious flights of visual fantasy. His music videos are near-seminal, works of art in their own right. A Lego-based stop-motion animation for The White Stripes' 'Fell In Love With A Girl' presented his fondness for filmmakers like Norman McLaren and Len Lye, while the immaculately synchronised dance routine which made up the video for Daft Punk's 'Around the World' harked back to the modernist choreography by Bob Fosse and Busby Berkeley. **DJ**

WHAT I LOVE ABOUT MOVIES

FEATURING

KRISTEN STEWART

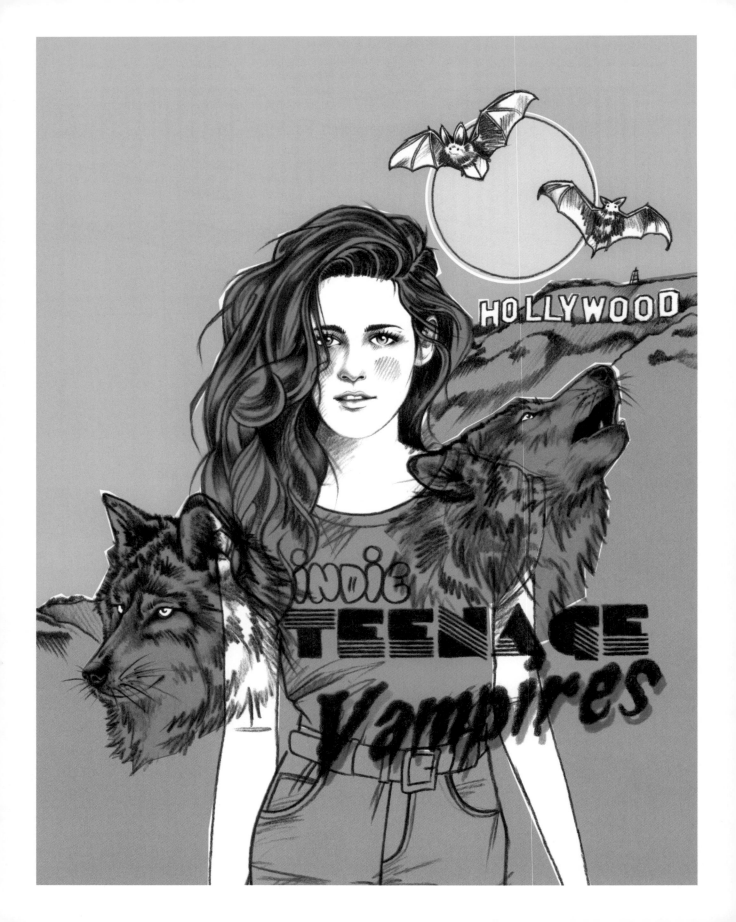

"I don't want to sound pretentious, but
I don't want to be in the entertainment
industry. I don't. I'm not a performer. I only
know I just want to do stories that are worth
being told. Not to make any grand statements
but it's like there's a kind of common good,
there's a common curiosity. It's like one step
beyond reading. Reading something, you do
get to experience it. But as an actor, you get
to personally get as close to that experience
as you possibly can. You actually,
literally, walk in their shoes."

Illustration by

RIK LEE

▼

Few would have predicted that Stephanie Meyer's Young Adult-oriented *Twilight* novels would go on to spawn one of the highest-grossing film series in the history of cinema (2008-12). Not least Kristen Stewart, who was thrust into the public consciousness in a cascade of flash bulbs and screaming internet fandom when she landed the lead role of Bella Swan. For Stewart, fame has always been a thorny issue. It's not that she's ungrateful for the adulation, the exposure and the financial security that her five-film stint as the 21st century's pre-eminent female literary icon has afforded her; more that international megastardom was never really on the agenda.

You only have to take a cursory glance at social media feeds and entertainment news sites to see the corruptive influence of fame on a Hollywood starlet. It's to Stewart's credit, then, that she's managed to keep her feet firmly on the ground. The movie star boyfriend with the model looks and the Beverly Hills mansion may come with the territory, but she is an unassuming idol driven by an insatiable desire to keep making the kinds of movies she loves. It's important to note that Stewart made her feature-length debut six years before *Twilight*, playing Jodie Foster's daughter in David Fincher's home-invasion thriller, *Panic Room* (2002). Stewart followed that with a string of eye-catching supporting roles, most notably in Sean Penn's *Into the Wild* and the low-budget horror *The Messengers*, both released in 2007.

Though she will always be synonymous with hair-gelled vampires and smooth-chested werehunks, Stewart is smart enough not to let *Twilight* become a career millstone. She regularly uses her star power to get smaller, more personal projects off the ground; she played against type as a wayward stripper in 2010's *Welcome to the Rileys* and later landed a dream role of Marylou in Walter Salles' adaptation of Jack Kerouac's Beat bible, *On the Road* (2012). Stewart is still prone to dipping her toe into blockbuster waters every now and then — she's reprising her eponymous role in the sequel to 2012's *Snow White and the Huntsman*. Even so, Stewart will always be an indie girl at heart. **AW**

WHAT I LOVE ABOUT MOVIES

FEATURING

ALEXANDER PAYNE

"People who love movies love people and love the planet, and, sort of, love gossip. We're limited by where we live, whom we know, where we are; we can only be in one place at one time doing one thing. Watching a movie transports you to a different time and place and story. It allows us to live vicariously, and we all want to live vicariously. We want to live many lives. We want to roll it all into one life. And if you can spy on someone else's life in a grandly entertaining way in two hours, what's better? We're so lucky to have lived in an era where cinema even exists. All those poor sons of bitches, billions of them, who lived and died and never got to see a movie. Don't that just make you wanna cry? We look to art as a sort of mirror to who we are, and cinema is the most verisimilar mirror. And another reason is that it's a way of conquering death. You can capture someone alive and refer to them for the rest of time. You watch all those old movies and you see someone long dead, that's pretty cool. And then there's the unconscious aspect to it; we love movies because of their relationship to dreams. Digital projection is cool and beautiful, but I miss the flicker of film. That's where the soul lies; in every circle and scratch mark."

Illustration by

PAUL BLOW

▼

This bookish and dry-witted Greek-American with an unfussy (some might call it deadpan) mode of storytelling chooses his films with care. His discerning nature has paid off on the award circuit and placed him in high regard among quality actors who, in Payne's words, "are reeled in because they want to play these parts". The parts in question embody the banality and humiliations of existence, observing American everymen (and women) whose lives are twisted and occasionally ruined by flash errors of judgement. Payne often reveals these crises in unflattering detail, but he makes certain that they're lined with a bracing ring of truth and empathy.

His cinematic breakthrough came in 1999 with *Election*, a story of petty high-school politicking which worked as an acerbic sister film to Wes Anderson's *Rushmore* from the previous year. Jack Nicholson was gifted one of his greatest late roles in *About Schmidt* (2002), a rueful road comedy about a cantankerous elderly gent coming to terms with the death of his wife. 2002's oenophile comedy *Sideways* (2004) had Paul Giamatti deliver the immortal line, "I am NOT drinking any fucking Merlot!" But *Nebraska*, from 2013, is unusual, and not just for its black-and-white photography; Payne didn't write a word of it, in contrast to his five previous directorial efforts. This latter quintet ranged from his 1996 debut, *Citizen Ruth*, an original screenplay written with Jim Taylor, to subsequent literary adaptations such as *The Descendants* (2011).

Payne is vocal about how much pleasure he gets from making movies and he values actors greatly, seeing them as much more than what he describes as, "circles to be moved around a screen". They are integral ingredients, second only to the script in importance. The complexity of human relations and how we come to terms with mortality are thematic preoccupations. *The Descendants* and *Nebraska* are clearly the products of an older, wiser director, someone who uses film to emphasise the subtle beauty the world has to offer while gently bemoaning our ability to take life, the people around us and the relationships we have with them, entirely for granted. **SMK**

ADMIT ONE
ONLY

WHAT I LOVE ABOUT MOVIES

FEATURING

DANIEL RADCLIFFE

"Movies can be anything. They can be escape or they can be confrontation. It's an incredibly malleable art form, which takes the best of every other art form — writing, music, performance, visual imagery. It's such a complete art at it's best. In terms of being on film sets, what I love about it is for anywhere between 20 and 260 days a band of complete strangers will come together and form a family, and will bring something beautiful and ordered out of that chaos."

Illustration by

SAM DUNN

Daniel Radcliffe will forever be synonymous with round specs and a lightning-bolt scar. But in the three years since the concluding part of the ludicrously successful wizarding mega franchise, the West London-born actor has shown that a long and prosperous career in the movies is well within his reach. Much like his long-serving co-star Emma Watson, Radcliffe has chosen his roles wisely post-*Potter*, coming of age in the high-brow Beat drama *Kill Your Darlings*, where he played a young Allen Ginsberg, and having already impressed as the lead in a 2012 adaptation of Susan Hill's Gothic horror novel 'The Woman in Black'.

Despite a reported net worth of around £56m ($93m), Radcliffe has maintained a low profile since his stratospheric rise, shrewdly swerving Potter-mania and the sort of gossip column conjecture commonly occupied by those who hit global stardom at such a tender age. There's a general assumption with child stars that their success has somehow been gifted to them; consequently, you'll find people willing them to fail and fade away. Radcliffe is acutely aware of this, and he's learned to deal with the speculation and expectation by quietly honing his craft. Radcliffe adopts an uncanny New Hampshire accent in the fantasy drama, *Horns* (2013), while his more recent credits include a major adaptation of Mary Shelley's *Frankenstein* as well as the hardboiled thriller, *Tokyo Vice* (2014).

Radcliffe has described his learning curve over the past few years as "very steep," and a headline-making performance in the 2007 production of *Equus*, which required the then 17-year-old Radcliffe to appear naked on stage, was an early indicator of his fearless approach to acting and an eagerness to learn. Eschewing social media and glitzy red carpet premieres has undoubtedly helped Radcliffe to handle his massive profile, but above all it's his enthusiasm, nerve and eye for a challenge that's keeping him on the right career path. **AW**

ADMIT ONE
ONLY

WHAT I LOVE ABOUT MOVIES

FEATURING

DANNY BOYLE

"What I love about movies I think is the dark room and you sit there with strangers. If you think about it psychologically... If somebody from another planet asked us, "What do you think psychologically about people who go and sit with a load of strangers in a dark room and watch 40-foot high versions of themselves kissing and shagging and hurting each other," you'd think, 'That's insane. They're mad those people, they're absolutely mad.' And I love the way we play our madness on it, really."

Illustration by

STEVEN WILSON

D anny Boyle is the last person that you could imagine making a workmanlike fist out of bringing bland material to the screen. "Hyperkinetic" is his rote aesthetic, especially when the premise makes that a seeming impossibility. *Trainspotting*, from 1996, focuses on heroin addicts whose sedentary activities seem to inherently lend themselves to recorded lethargy, but Boyle's second feature (after his 1994 black comedy debut *Shallow Grave*) confirmed early on that, even in the unlikeliest of circumstances, he feels the shark-like imperative to stay in constant motion or die.

With his relentless need for speed, Boyle would seem a natural England-to-Hollywood transplant, yet his two stabs at straight studio work (1997's *A Life Less Ordinary* and 2001's *The Beach*) both underperformed critically and commercially. A surfeit of resource appeared to slow him down, but with 2002's scrappier *28 Days Later...*, Boyle reinvigorated both himself and the then-moribund zombie genre — naturally, by making the living dead jog at a relay-winning trot rather than the usual lurching suffle.

Boyle followed up with the underappreciated *Millions* (2004), a typically swift but uncharacteristic stab at family cinema. Then it was back to violence and adrenalised fear: 2007's *Sunshine* took a standard crisis-in-space scenario and used the imminent possibility of the end of the world as an excuse to scream at deafening volume into the void. The following year's *Slumdog Millionaire* was even more emphatic, visually slicing and dicing Mumbai into a world of relentless violence, a melodrama that pummelled young protagonist Dev Patel with sadistically overwhelming odds until delivering him to a hard-earned happy ending and a comparatively laidback Bollywood number.

For 2010 follow-up *127 Hours*, Boyle faced being hemmed in by the premise of a mountain climber whose arm is trapped between a rock and the wall of a deep gully. But by following the internal mental thought processes of James Franco's frantic adventurer he found another reasonable excuse for stylistic hyperventilation. By this point, more part of the British film establishment than young gun, Boyle was recruited to present the UK to the world in the opening ceremony of the 2012 Olympic Games. His typically unstately response was to have James Bond parachute from a helicopter, apparently attached to the Queen of England. **VR**

WHAT I LOVE ABOUT MOVIES

FEATURING

VIGGO MORTENSEN

"The places you will go."

Illustration by

LUKE BROOKES

Viggo Mortensen made his film debut at the age of 27, lurking in the margins of Peter Weir's 1985 film *Witness*. A late start and his default, beady-eyed glare made him an unlikely candidate for a second act rise to leading man prominence; he looked set for a career of villains and eccentric character turns, at best. But amid the bloated fantasy murk of *Lord Of The Rings* (2001-2003), Mortensen's sword-wielding warrior purified the pre-fab portent around him. Not a performer for half measures, Mortensen carried his blade in and out of character, his lean frame tilting into a heavy stride to reflect the toll of constantly bearing the tools of his trade.

Unsure how to employ an actor with a body capable of mayhem but without the explicit brawn or belligerence of a Schwarzenegger or Stallone, Hollywood put Mortensen astride a horse in *Hidalgo* (2004) and hoped he could carry an anachronistic desert adventure on his own. Audiences weren't having it. Enter David Cronenberg, a director previously not noted for using the same actors over and over. In 2005's *A History Of Violence*, Mortensen is an unlikely-looking family man, his wary watchfulness reflecting an awareness of the coiled potential for violence not shared by his sedentary Midwestern community. The actor reveals his true self when bloodshed comes to his café, and from that point his body's latent capability and character's actions are in terrifying sync. Human flesh has often nurtured infection and terror in Cronenberg's films, but Mortensen's lean vitality is even more frightening, enabling reflexive, unthinking havoc.

For a follow-up, Cronenberg had Mortensen strip down to the ball-slapping nude for a bathhouse knife fight as a credible Russian mob enforcer in 2007's *Eastern Promises*, then clothed him as Sigmund Freud in *A Dangerous Method*. Casually tri-lingual and openly impatient with Hollywood's tightening noose of possibilities, the actor has ventured into Spanish-language work, becoming the unlikely monetary draw for determinedly arthouse-oriented Argentinian Lisandro Alonso's forthcoming fifth film. Even if Hollywood never finds another appropriate role for him, Mortensen seems happy to settle into his role as an eccentric polymath along the lines of a kinder, gentler Vincent Gallo, supervising his *Lord of the Rings*-enabled boutique publishing house and releasing marginal music projects.**VR**

WHAT I LOVE ABOUT MOVIES

FEATURING

JULIETTE BINOCHE

"I've been very lucky in my career and I'm even luckier to still have huge passion for what I do. I've always enjoyed working with people from the world, with different minds and visions and stories to tell. I'm very proud of so many of my films, and I love adapting to new scenarios and new ways of working. I've never been a 9-5 person, I love the freedom of cinema. I love the anarchy."

Illustration by
KAREENA ZEREFOS

Juliette Binoche is an actor who puts paid to the notion that auteur theory is reserved exclusively for the work of directors. Though Binoche has collaborated with some of the world's greatest living filmmakers (her Rolodex includes Abbas Kiarostami, Hou Hsiao-hsien, Michael Haneke and Bruno Dumont), the films in which she stars are as much "Juliette Binoche" movies as they are examples of sublime directorial artistry. She was discovered back in 1985 by no less than Jean-Luc Godard where she was cast as a Mary Magdelene manqué in his re-contextualising of the birth of Christ in modern-day Switzerland, *Hail Mary*. (20 years later, she reprised the role for Abel Ferrara in his underrated 2005 film, *Mary*). In an interview with *Film Comment* magazine, Binoche spoke of how working with Godard was not all that she had envisioned, particularly in the way he rejected any kind of patriarchal relationship with her. It was only until later that year when Binoche would emerge as a fully-fledged leading lady, playing a young actress on the hunt for stardom in Andre Techine's noir-ish erotic drama, *Rendez-Vous*. The potency and fervour she brought to her screen work was palpable from the off, as if she was employing intricate "method"-style performance manoeuvres to formulate characters not far removed from her natural persona.

Though occasionally ushered in as a sprightly emblem of French feistiness in such titles as Lasse Hallström's *Chocolat* (2000) and Anthony Mingella's *The English Patient* (1996), her finest work can be found in the films where she is able to directly channel feelings and experiences from her own professional and personal life. Arguably her greatest screen moment can be found in Michael Haneke's masterful 2000 film, *Code Unknown*, a lightly experimental examination of racial, class and gender estrangement in modern Europe. She plays an actor auditioning for a role, shown standing in a dark room while, from behind a DV camera, an unseen director (played by Haneke) tells her she's going to die. Her intense reaction makes for extremely uncomfortable viewing, and the scene as a whole beautifully encapsulates the strange and emotionally draining travails of a screen actor, the Machiavellian hand of the director, and Binoche's own sublime skill for creating hyperreal variants of real-life characters who retain a sense of palpable and rugged empathy. **DJ**

ADMIT ONE
ONLY

WHAT I LOVE ABOUT MOVIES

• FEATURING •

HARMONY KORINE

"I don't know, I just love 'em. I like...
It's hard, it's like asking, 'What do you like
about magic?' I like going to other places,
experiencing other things. I always liked
them as a kid. I probably like them because
I can't describe why I like them."

Illustration by

DILRAJ MANN

Perhaps one of the most mischievous, wantonly divisive directors working in America today, Harmony Korine has built a tidy career on the subversive art of finely-calibrated needling and arch provocation. Cat lovers ran from the stalls in 1997 as his lauded/reviled directorial debut, *Gummo*, unspooled to unwitting revellers; a ramshackle rummage through the human detritus of a hurricane-battered Ohio town. Within minutes of the film starting, two teenagers are seen harvesting cats with BB guns in order to sell the meat to a local Chinese restaurant. Korine himself takes great pride in obfuscation, a teller of tall tales rather than a man who abides by the traditional truth-telling methods of the conservative media. He found himself doing the TV chatshow rounds (in what felt like some strange Dadaist stunt) following the release of Larry Clark's realist/nihilist ode to dangerously untethered youth, *Kids*, for which he supplied the script.

Much like Denmark's Lars von Trier, there's an intrinsic sense of morbid intrigue with Korine's work which even extreme naysayers would be hard-pressed to deny. His work appears on some levels as bullishly anti-intellectual and combative, and yet on others there's evidence of carefully aligned cerebral subtexts and the feeling that the work in question is more considered and more enigmatic than it initially appears. The experimental 2009 video comedy, *Trash Humpers*, was dismissed by many as a pale imitation of the stunt-based TV show *Jackass*. It saw a hollering trio of rubber-masked OAPs live out violent fantasies for a juddering camera. Korine himself said he wanted the film to feel like something that was found in a dumpster; with that, its status as a strange artistic artefact grew.

His (again, highly divisive) 2012 film, *Spring Breakers*, appeared on paper to be an unapologetic sortie into the mainstream, with his top-line stars consisting of ex-cast members from Disney's *High School Musical* plus James Franco as a grill-toothed gangsta rapper. It's a slippery movie, and not necessarily in a bad way. Its fundamental genius (if that's the right word) lies in its ambiguity. *Spring Breakers* is as easy to read as a giant, neon-gilded prank which the film's own stars might not even be intellectually party to, as it is an earnest, Fellini-esque celebration of extreme corporeal debasement and, by extension, the end of days. **DJ**

WHAT I LOVE ABOUT MOVIES

FEATURING

CASEY AFFLECK

"I think that, for me, films have a unique ability to transport the viewer to a different place. I see people staring at a painting in a museum for five hours and they seem lost in some experience. But I've never been that way. I grew up watching movies and it's movies that... They move me. And they excite me."

Illustration by
OLIVER STAFFORD

To many it was a long time coming. Casey Affleck finally stepped out of his older brother's shadow in 2007 with the blistering double-header of *Gone Baby Gone* and *The Assassination of Jesse James by the Coward Robert Ford*. The latter earned him an Academy Award nomination, but, while film critics were busy heaping praise on the then 32-year-old actor, Affleck was casually distancing himself from the hype. Truth is, red carpets and champagne ceremonies never really suited him, his reluctant-movie-star demeanour more like a sincere affectation. Affleck is an actor who defines himself by his (often unexpected) career choices. He injects a little bit of his personality into every character he plays, and his deep affection for language and the written word — he cites Atticus Finch, John Grady Cole and Odysseus as literary heroes — will always lure him towards more cultured ventures.

Affleck has been obsessed with watching movies for as long as he can remember. At 10 he moved to Mexico with his family for a year, during which time he recalls having access to only four VHS tapes; the only one that interested him being *Romancing the Stone* (1984), which he watched over a dozen times. While stationed south of the border Affleck became fluent in Spanish, a skill he would put to good use in Steven Soderbergh's 2007 film *Ocean's Thirteen*: in a scene set in a Mexican factory that required Affleck to don a cracking handlebar moustache.

Affleck's first big role came in 1995's *To Die For*, in which he played a sociopathic teenager alongside Nicole Kidman and Joaquin Phoenix. During filming, Affleck and Phoenix formed a close bond that has had a significant impact on both actors' professional and personal lives. Phoenix introduced Affleck to his sister, Summer, and the pair married in 2006. It was Phoenix, too, who provided a vital contribution to Affleck's directorial debut, the 2010 meta mockumentary-cum-performance-art caper, *I'm Still Here*. This widely discussed and controversial prank united critics in acclamation; a surprising twist that echoes Affleck's enigmatic appeal. **AW**

WHAT I LOVE ABOUT MOVIES

FEATURING

WES ANDERSON

"Um... yeah... That's a big one. I think, umm... Well, it's interesting. [pause] I can separate it into two things. One thing that happens to me is that so often we watch movies on DVD or Blu-ray or you're on the train and you're watching it on a mini iPad. But I will say that when I find myself back in the movie theatre, once I've slogged through – in France – 25 minutes of advertisements, and the thing finally begins, I still have that feeling: ahh, it's beginning! Even if three minutes later I'm sat there thinking, God damn, we shouldn't even be here! There is something about the feeling of someone casting a spell and taking you completely out of your life and putting you in some other place that would be very difficult to get to any other way. That's the thing I've always loved the most about movies, being transported some place else. The other thing I'll say is that lately I've been watching a lot of movies from the pre-code Hollywood era. There's a lot of movies I love from that time, but I've never thought I wanted to sit down and watch this specific set of movies. I've watched dozens and dozens of these. It's a different experience in a way, because I feel that when you're watching them at home, you're doing a kind of survey. Even though these movies are entertaining, there's something academic about watching them in this way. I'm asking myself constantly, how did they do it? And what is making these movies so different from the movies that came four years later? What happened? In this way, it's less the act of being transported and more like they're the most complex, strange little objects that still exist from this time. They combine and capture actual life. All these different artists doing their separate thing simultaneously. I've had several conversations with people where I've asked them why these movies are different. I have a friend in New York who's a real film scholar and he gave me a definitive answer as to why they're different. And none of it, to me, captures what makes these movies different. There's something about them that you can't... They're so complex that it would be impossible to break down. I don't know. I'm not sure if re-reading what I've just said I could entirely stand behind it, but those are my two answers."

Illustration by

ANDREW FAIRCLOUGH

The willingness of Bill Murray to sport a pair of loose-fitting, Budweiser-emblazoned swimming shorts, lackadaisically toss golf-balls into a dank pool before himself taking the plunge was arguably the scene that placed Wes Anderson a good head-and-shoulders above the tranche of try-hard '90s indie-school filmmakers. 1998's *Rushmore* was the director's second feature, about an overzealous working-class teen (Jason Schwartzman) attending a prestigious private school and habitually prizing extracurricular activities over academic learning. The film didn't merely showcase Anderson's hyper-fastidious directorial mode, his fondness for forcibly juxtaposing the archaic and the modern, and his close affinity with the writing of JD Salinger. It also established him as a rare director able to create ostensibly comic films with an undertow of deep melancholy. His first, 1996's *Bottle Rocket*, had slipped by largely unnoticed due to marketeers' attempts to sell the film as a roistering, geeky homage to *Reservoir Dogs*. In hindsight, it remains a stellar debut.

Though hardly what you'd call a runaway box-office success, *Rushmore* opened the door to far more expansive, intricate and idiosyncratic projects, all of which tend to orbit around the concept of family and its various philosophical adjuncts. Gene Hackman, Ben Stiller, Gwyneth Paltrow and long-time collaborator Owen Wilson came aboard *The Royal Tenenbaums* (2001), which depicted the psychological traumas of parental expectation and exposed the myth of natural familial intimacy. The strains of the personal and the professional littered the bobble-hatted seafaring caper, *The Life Aquatic With Steve Zissou* (2004), a film which took colourful inspiration from the '60s oceanography films of Jacques Cousteau. During his more recent work, Anderson's style has shifted further into the domain of the animated picturebook, with films like 2012's *Moonrise Kingdom* and 2014's *The Grand Budapest Hotel* referencing the 2D silhouette animation of German director Lotte Reiniger. Anderson's predilection for drawing together gigantic ensemble casts posits him as some kind of itinerant and lovably eccentric father figure to the acting elite of Hollywood and Europe. In person, he is often seen sporting trademark vintage tweed suits or beige-brown corduroy. **DJ**

ADMIT ONE
ONLY

WHAT I LOVE ABOUT MOVIES

FEATURING

MIA WASIKOWSKA

▼

"It's a universal language and there are few things that are so powerful. It's an immersive experience, but you can learn so much about different places and cultures and that's accessible to everybody - whether people choose to go see those movies or a blockbuster is a different thing, but either way it's entertainment or a cultural experience, so it provides so many things."

Illustration by
ELEANOR TAYLOR

The actor Mia Wasikowska rose to prominence by essaying young women with an innate strangeness bubbling behind their eyes. Her training as a ballerina has given the Australian a straight-backed poise which, added to translucent skin-colouring and exquisite bone structure, creates an ethereal glow distinct from conventional Hollywood beauties. She is striking enough to be a viable lead, but just odd enough to excel as a meaningful side-player without coming across as a shoehorned-in starlet.

Tim Burton cast her as Alice in his 3D rendering of *Alice In Wonderland* (2010) and she wasn't shy about expressing her empathy, saying in an interview with *Harper's Bazaar* magazine, that "Alice has a certain discomfort within herself, within society and among her peers; I have definitely felt similarly." Whenever she is on a screen, whatever she's doing, or saying - even if it's very little – Wasikowska seems on edge, ready to explode. Her big roles, from classic downtrodden heroine in *Jane Eyre* (2011) to budding emo-sociopath in Park Chan-wook's *Stoker* (2013), have showcased her uncanny mastery for quietly reacting to violent surroundings – a gift that appears to come from deep within. This child of photographer parents uses creative work to get to personal truth and vice versa.

The role that, at 18 years old, made her name in America was the antithesis to these self-possessed types. Anorexic gymnast, Sophie, in the HBO psychologist drama *In Treatment* (2008) was articulate, hateful and enmeshed with her own auto-destruction. She was a poster child for teenage angst, a more pathological Holden Caulfield with an added X chromosome.

She is emerging as the go-to gal for international arthouse directors who have cottoned on to her live-wire intrigue. Jim Jarmusch, Richard Ayoade, David Cronenberg and Guillermo del Toro have recently cast the busy 24-year-old who seems happy to have found a position in the industry which makes her something of a beacon for actresses who favour complex characters. Her rich talents have secured the attention of the indie glitterati, but she also has a thoughtful head on her young shoulders: Wasikowska reads literature on set, is a photographer and has directed *The Long, Clear View*, a chapter in Australian film portmanteau, *The Turning* (2013). *Maps to the Stars* (2014) is the David Cronenberg Hollywood satire in which she stars with Robert Pattinson; perhaps the title is a metaphor for how her career will continue to progress. **SMK**

ADMIT ONE
ONLY

WHAT I LOVE ABOUT MOVIES

FEATURING

WILLIAM FRIEDKIN

"Film is the most important art form created in the twentieth century. Film presents an opportunity to present ideas, largely visually but also through dialogue. That just wasn't something people could do 150 years ago, and it's provided creative people with an outlet for their thoughts and passions in a way that is totally different to painting a picture or writing a book. Most art forms require isolation. You create solely alone, standing in front of a canvas with a brush or some paint. Or you're sat in front of a blank piece of paper with a typewriter or a pen for company. As a filmmaker, you have to use what we call a one-ton pencil, which is a vast crew of people to whom you must communicate and express your ideas and the images in your mind and the way they move and combine. I see it and value it as an extraordinary artform and the best forum for ideas in the larger public realm."

Illustration by
HEDOF

The shock effect of the impetuous violence in William Friedkin's career/reputation-making '70s one-two punch — 1971's *The French Connection*, 1973's *The Exorcist* — has diminished with time. Belying his background in documentary, those films often seemed to cast Friedkin more as a frustrated procedural filmmaker forcing himself to work within genre frameworks than someone spoiling to get a rise out of viewers by any means necessary. Much of *Connection* is tense, wordless surveillance work; an excuse for extensive NYC location shooting punctuated rather than defined by its famed car-vs-subway chase. Likewise, in *The Exorcist*, Friedkin seemed far more interested in the nuts and bolts of period brain scan technology than the Catholic bad-seed drama in which these scenes were embedded.

Friedkin earned a reputation as one of the most uncontrollable and self-destructively indulgent '70s filmmakers with the endless, expensive production of 1977's *Sorcerer*. That perception was both accurate and essentially irrelevant to those not obliged to finance him. The dated narrative obscured his considerable technical strengths and refusal to turn away from potentially unpleasant material. An increasing willingness to do anything for effect has merged uneasily throughout his career with a gift for constructing and capturing down-and-out people and places. This fascination has often been indistinguishable from endorsement: Matthew McConaughey's Killer Joe (in the 2012 film of the same name) is a violent psychotic and the charismatic centre of any room he enters. Friedkin's films are troubling (although not always in the ways he seems to think), but the standard tale of his '70s hubris obscures his considerable, nerve-wracking gifts.

It's the rare non-oversimplification in film history to say that Friedkin truly invented the editorial rules of the modern (now sadly antiquarian) car chase in *The French Connection*, a feat revisited and one-upped in 1985's *To Live And Die In LA*. It's also true that in shooting that landmark, Friedkin worked without permits and endangered lives. The chase is Friedkin's specialty, and he doesn't need automobiles to pull it off – 2003's undervalued *The Hunted* is as excessively, unquestioningly macho as any of his earlier works, steeped in textbook laconic brutality. It's also an anthology of brilliant on-foot chases, the camera as speedy and unshakeably focused as its subjects. **VR**

WHAT I LOVE ABOUT MOVIES

FEATURING

TSAI MING-LIANG

"[*long pause*] Hmm [*long pause*] What they tell us about life. It's a strange medium. We watch movies. We know they are not real, but we think they are. We think they reflect life. Actually, what they reflect is inner-life. [*pause*] I also like to think that cinema has a life of its own."

Illustration by

JENSINE ECKWALL

If the Malaysia-born, Taiwan-based director Tsai Ming-liang is to be fully believed, when the apocalypse finally arrives, it will be water-based. And it could come in the form of rain, floods, leaky taps, stagnant rivers, jacuzzis, plumbing blunders, frozen food or even watermelons. One of the world's leading exponents of "slow cinema" and the immaculately composed long take, Tsai's soporific, near-mute characters lope through the frame and react to their surroundings as if submerged in a giant water tank. How do humans respond to this unstoppable deluge of liquid? As Tsai would have it, they quietly weep, their streams of tears poetically, ironically adding to the tide.

There's an overriding sense of pessimism in Tsai's work, and yet his cinema offers a vision of the fractured, delicate beauty – or musicality – nestled amid the ruins of modern society. 2003's *Goodbye Dragon Inn* is a deadpan, real-time portrait of a Taipei picture palace 90 minutes prior to its permanent closure. The oddball scattering of farewell patrons drift through the grand location like disoriented, sad-eyed apparitions, as the film itself whispers an eloquent, rueful lament for the death of this apparently antiquated mode of communal activity.

Films like *Vive L'Amour* (1994), *The Wayward Cloud* (2005) and *The Hole* (1998) examine the problems that come of people living together in confined spaces and the sense of alienation that not only exists, but is exacerbated by the architecture of sprawling, urban apartment blocks. Actor Lee Kang-sheng, Tsai's collaborator, muse and on-screen avatar, has featured in every one of his films (often as lead) since his 1992 debut, *Rebels of the Neon God*. As a performer, Lee usually embraces the extreme outskirts of Zen-like calm and violent fury, seldom opting for the bland middle ground. His bottle-rocket intensity can best be surveyed in the 1997 masterpiece, *The River*, as he essays a hapless film extra who contracts a strange infection in the form of a sore neck after agreeing to wade into a polluted river for the camera. The film is as much a literal examination of urban desolation as it is a commentary on the hazardous emotional and physical strains of moviemaking.

At the 2013 Venice Film Festival, Tsai informally announced his retirement, suggesting that his extraordinary film *Stray Dogs* – a heartbreaking study of life on Tapei's economic fringes captured as a compendium of haunting long takes – might be his swansong. He then went on to make the scintilating "slow cinema" essay, *Journey to the West*, with Lee and chameleonic French actor Denis Lavant, so who really knows? **DJ**

ADMIT ONE
ONLY

WHAT I LOVE ABOUT MOVIES

· FEATURING ·

PHILIP SEYMOUR HOFFMAN

▼

"Umm... I think... that... I don't know, I think that there's something that touches you when you go to the movies, you kind of get sucked into this dream state. There's something that happens when you're in a dark room watching something that has a certain impact on you that reaches a very deep, subconscious part of you. It's indelible. It stays with you for a long time. I think that's why when you go back and watch a film that you loved from when you were younger it's never quite the same experience. Even though it's the exact same film. In the theatre you're not in a dark room, and there's a sense of interaction that you don't get with being in a cinema. It's a very communal experience, but cinema is isolated, it's just for you and it affects you on a much deeper level in that sense."

Illustration by

RAID71

F ew actors commanded the respect and reverence given to Philip Seymour Hoffman throughout his illustrious and tragically curtailed career. An actor first and a movie star second, Hoffman's ability to switch gears without compromising his awesome reputation saw him hop seamlessly and gracefully between the mainstream (2006's *Mission: Impossible III*, 2013's *The Hunger Games: Catching Fire*) and challenging independent productions (2008's *Synecdoche, New York* 2007's *Before the Devil Knows You're Dead*). Whatever the size, scale or genre, however, Hoffman possessed the simple ability to make every film he was in a little better.

Hoffman delivered arguably his finest screen performance in what was one of his final films, Paul Thomas Anderson's sumptuous and surreal post-war drama, *The Master* (2012), for which he received his fourth Academy Award nomination. And it was with Anderson that Hoffman shone brightest. Since PTA's 1996 debut, *Hard Eight*, Hoffman featured in all but one of the writer/director's five features — the exception being 2007's *There Will Be Blood*. But it is his bewitching portrayal of charismatic cult leader Lancaster Dodd in *The Master* that surely cemented his legacy.

News of Hoffman's death in early February 2014 sparked an overwhelming emotional response from the world media, with former colleagues, long-term admirers and general well-wishers lining up to pay tribute. As one of the most cherished actors of his generation, the emphatic posthumous praise was fully justified. A self-proclaimed "theatre guy" who joined the New York theatre company LAByrinth in 1995, later becoming its co-artistic director, Hoffman arrived surprisingly late on the movie scene. It wasn't until Hoffman was in his mid-twenties that auditions started going his way — he followed up small supporting roles in *Scent of a Woman* (1992) and *The Getaway* (1994) with profile-raising parts in gale-force thriller, *Twister* (1996), and Paul Thomas Anderson's porno saga/satire, *Boogie Nights* (1997). Within a decade Hoffman was being toasted at the 78th Academy Awards for his powerhouse turn in the 2005 biopic, *Capote*, bringing a Truman Capote to the screen who was more than merely a collection of precious actorly tics and a well-maintained accent. That you could make a case for so many of Hoffman's performances being his greatest is testament to both supreme range and a remarkable consistency. His rise was meteoric, and his star unlikely to fade. **AW**

WHAT I LOVE ABOUT MOVIES

FEATURING

SHANE CARRUTH

"Movies are the height of narrative right now. Right now, the thing that most excites me about film is that I don't think it's found its true form yet. Or at least I think there's a form that it could take, a way movies could be used that we haven't got to yet. I'm really passionate about trying to figure that out. I think movies could be much more experiential, much more densely packed, much more compelling, much more lyrical, much more musical. I hope I'm around long enough to figure that out."

Illustration by
DIEGO PATIÑO

Why expend time, effort and wads of cash expanding digital cinematic forms when everything we could ever need is right here in front of our noses? Such is the working remit of filmmaker and polymath Shane Carruth, an artist who sees possibilities for the sublime in everyday items such as self-assembly shelving units, household pot plants and piglets. Lots of piglets. His career arc thus far does not conform to the Hollywood norm. Since 2004, he has made just two movies. His first, *Primer* from 2004, was a shock to the system, a chilling micro-budget science fiction movie that played like Marker's *La Jetée* (1962). It dared to speculate: what if two regular guys with a keen interest in science invented time travel in their garage? In many ways, this was what Carruth was doing with this movie – thinking beyond his meagre budgetary perimeters and proving that huge, mind-melting ideas could be packaged and produced quickly, cheaply, successfully and brilliantly.

Such is his violently idiosyncratic vision and militant desire to only make the movies he wants to make, it took another nine years for Carruth to return to our screens, but he did so in spectacular style. Written, directed, edited, produced, photographed and scored by Carruth, 2013's *Upstream Colour* took his concept of organic fantasy to an insane new plateau. A markedly straightforward narrative concerning a man and a woman discovering that they have both been the victim of an elaborate, mind-warping ruse involving narcotic grubs(!) is shrouded in mystery via discursive episodes, dreamy asides and diffuse editing. At no point does the filmmaker offer any explanation as to what the film is about.

In person, Carruth is similarly inscrutable. Happy to talk technique, the particulars of funding a movie and the daily difficulties of working as a truly independent artist, he knows that his movies would be rendered meaningless were he to divulge their true meaning. He tried for years to get a sci-fi epic with the none-too-commercial title of *A Topiary* off the ground; even with Steven Soderbergh and David Fincher as executive producers, the funding never arrived. He now has another project on the slate. It's called *The Modern Ocean* and is said to concern the science and profitability of shipping lanes. What it's actually about, we'll have to wait, see and then probably decide for ourselves. **DJ**

ADMIT ONE
ONLY

WHAT I LOVE ABOUT MOVIES

FEATURING

TOM HARDY

"I don't know... I love to disappear into different worlds. I love people's work. I love to see good work. I love to be able to disappear into a film. If I can't disappear into a film then I end up talking through it and I don't enjoy it. As soon as I shut up, you know I've enjoyed it. In the house I used to live in many years ago, we each had a Native American nickname. It was kind of a dumb joke. So our dog was called 'Lives in Hope', my flatmate, who is an extremely loud person, was called 'He Who Talks Through Walls' and my name was 'He Who Talks Through Movies'. If I'm not talking, it means I'm inside the film and I remember every word, every detail. That's what I enjoy the most: disappearing. It makes me feel like a kid again."

Illustration by
JAMES WILSON

▼

Few actors are as intense in the flesh as they appear on screen. Tom Hardy is an exception to that rule. Meeting Hardy is like stepping into the ring with a prize fighter with one arm tied behind your back. Keep your guard up long enough, though, and the penetrating stare and imposing frame eventually appear to soften. Hardy's reputation may be rooted in a high-energy brand of wild-eyed machismo, but there's a vulnerable side to this British acting heavyweight. Hardy has experienced first-hand what bottoming out feels like, having come perilously close to sabotaging his career when an early fame spike went to his head. By his own admission, he's a better actor and person now. The ugly experience has made him more humble, kept him grounded and focused.

Today, Hardy is one of British cinema's most in-demand exports, having established himself as a brazen scene-stealer in Christopher Nolan's multi-layered sci-fi blockbuster, *Inception* (2010), and Tomas Alfredson's *Tinker Tailor Soldier Spy* (2011), and more recently landing meaty central roles in John Hillcoat's *Lawless* (2012) and Nolan's *The Dark Knight Rises* (2012), where he went toe-to-toe with Christian Bale's Caped Crusader as hoarse-voiced supervillain supremo, Bane. Hardy owes it all, he says, to a close friend and a brilliant script that spent years on the pre-production merry-go-round before Hardy's tooth-and-nail persistence finally paid off. Had Hardy failed in his efforts to convince Danish filmmaker Nicolas Winding Refn to cast him as the lead in 2009's biographical prison opera, *Bronson*, his career may well have flatlined. But, Hardy being Hardy, failure was never an option.

Every time he gets knocked down, Hardy rises stronger. Tell him he can't do something and he'll put himself through the wringer just to prove you wrong — say, packing on 13kg of solid muscle to portray an MMA fighter in 2011's *Warrior*. So, while he can come across as spiky, confrontational even, Hardy makes no apologies for wearing his emotions on his sleeve. His fear of throwing it all away keeps him looking ahead; if he manages to stay on his current trajectory then, excitingly, the best is probably yet to come. **AW**

ADMIT ONE
ONLY

WHAT I LOVE ABOUT MOVIES

· FEATURING ·

TERENCE DAVIES

"I love their magic. In a crowded room, in the dark, you watch something collectively but you think the secrets are being told only to you. That's magic."

Illustration by

SAM PASH

A single frame from Terence Davies' 1992 masterpiece *The Long Day Closes* has been co-opted by cinema houses and film chains across the globe as a simple way to capture the widely-held and brazenly romantic notion of movies as a conduit for sublime escape. The frame comprises a head-on shot of young Liverpudlian scamp Bud (played by the actor Leigh McCormack) staring sharply over a gilded balcony as a giant plume of white light emanates from behind him. When placing this shot into the context of the film at large, Davies' intentions are less benign: Bud is plagued by loneliness (physical, spiritual and sexual), one of life's hapless bystanders, frightened, confused and unwilling to roll with the tide.

The same could be said of Davies himself, one of the UK's greatest living directors and a man whose personal and professional lives have never been entirely in sync with the demands of the mainstream. His interests – music, movies, books, poetry – tend to centre on works produced before 1960, with TS Eliot's 'Four Quartets' often cited as his primary creative cornerstone. Yet while the artistic loves of his life remain unabashedly anachronistic, the formal qualities of his movies – the editing, the narrative structures, the playful use of pop and classical music – are defiantly modern and, on occasion, even tip into the realms of the experimental.

Davies is an auteur in the classical sense that, even when adapted from literary sources, his films are clearly statements of personal intent. 1988's quixotic reminiscence of 1950's working class Liverpool, *Distant Voices, Still Lives*, was directly inspired by his own childhood, with the late Pete Postlethwaite on rare form as his abusive toerag of a father. Yet, with his later cycle of tragic "women's pictures", *The House of Mirth* (based on Edith Wharton) and *The Deep Blue Sea* (based on Terence Rattigan), he managed to create dramas that could be taken both at face value, and as metaphors for his own disquiets about love, status and the inherent tragedy of existence. Consider Davies sitting on that balcony, the mighty projection beam his shelter from life's inexorable pageant of shame and sadness. **DJ**

WHAT I LOVE ABOUT MOVIES

· FEATURING ·

PARK CHAN-WOOK

"Expressions. The expressions on different people's faces. Watching expressions is, for me, the joy of watching films. To be able to look at the expressions on the faces of people from all over the world, from across all different times in history, from different cultures and ethnicities and from different social classes is a remarkable thing. With movies I get to see the faces of people I never would have otherwise met. And I can see a range of emotions expressed in their faces. Even if it's a shot where you can only see the back of a person's head and from very far away, you still have the satisfaction of imagining the expression they have on their faces. That's the joy of cinema."

Illustration by
ELENA GUMENIUK

Quentin Tarantino aside, no modern director has expressed such a continued yen for the gruesome, '70s-style mechanics of the revenge saga than South Korea's Park Chan-wook. He's a filmmaker who displays a formal rigour of near-clockwork precision. He neatly dovetails labyrinthine plots that transcend the bounds of implausibility with a grim, philosophical inevitability. It was in fact Tarantino who became one of Park's early boosters, awarding his film *OldBoy* the Grand Prix at the 2004 Cannes Film Festival. The film sees a drunken office stooge randomly incarcerated in a wallpapered cell for 15 years, then upon his release given three days to work out why.

Some chalked the film up as a *succès de scandale*, down to such Grand Guignol flourishes as lead actor, Choi Min-sik, eating a live squid as its tendrils continue to writhe over his face, and later a single, horizontal tracking shot in which Choi's character dispatches an entire army of goons with a claw-hammer. Yet its brutality is fundamental to its themes, as Park is less interested in the base morality of revenge than he is in exploring the operatic ways in which to orchestrate this revenge. *OldBoy* is the middle segment of a trilogy, which began with 2002's *Sympathy For Mr Vengeance*, about a man who is horribly duped by black market organ dealers, and 2005's *Lady Vengeance*, about a woman wrongly imprisoned for murder and out to locate the real perpetrator.

There's a contingent of Western critics who consider South Korean cinema too unremittingly bleak and violent. On a superficial level, Park's cinema does offer the haters their most cogent test case. Yet much of the violence in Park's cinema is laced with irony and presented as gaudy fantasy that's been facilitated by the artifice of cinema. 2006's underrated *I'm a Cyborg, But That's OK* enclosed a twentysomething rom-com within the confines of a mental institution, and duly offered hyper-violent visualisations of the patients' most base urges. The popularity of Park's work saw him direct his first English language work in 2013, a stylised slice of Hitchcockian gothic entitled *Stoker* starring Mia Wasikowska, Nicole Kidman and Matthew Goode. **DJ**

WHAT I LOVE ABOUT MOVIES

FEATURING

ALFONSO CUARÓN

▼

"As we go through the mystery of existence, films can't make us feel less lonely, but they can make us feel that it is okay to be alone."

▼

Mexico's Alfonso Cuarón has always been a director of some repute, but it took the release of his 2013 film, *Gravity*, for the world to finally buck up and take note. A labour of love which was many Moons in the making, this claustrophobic celestial two-hander set Sandra Bullock and George Clooney mercilessly adrift in high orbit, jerry-rigging an immaculately executed disaster movie around an eloquent meditation on mortality and the fragility of existence.

Cuarón's first major success as a "name" director arrived with the Spanish-language sex comedy/road-movie, *Y Tu Mamá También*, a frank and freewheeling exploration of Oedipal longing and stifled sexual peccadillos. A nucleus of subtle subversion has always been present in Cuarón's movies, and he is a director who appears unwilling and unable to toady to the generic strictures of the Hollywood production line. He's even able to wriggle and squirm when clamped in the tightest shackles possible, responsible as he is for making easily the best of the Harry Potter movies with *Harry Potter and the Prisoner of Azkaban*. Where the series as a whole existed as giant narrative fragments in an over-arching saga, Cuarón deviously produced a movie which miraculously worked on its own terms. And this without the assistance of his cinematographic partner-in-crime, Emmanuel Lubezki, who has been a Cuarón collaborator since the director's 1991 feature debut, *Love in the Time of Hysteria*.

What's especially interesting about the relationship between Lubezki and Cuarón is that the pair push one another creatively – Cuarón has said in interviews that Lubezki's initial solution for attaining the correct light when filming *Gravity* was to take the entire crew up to the International Space Station. One can trace the evolution of the sinuous long take that occupies the opening 17 minutes of *Gravity* back to *Prisoner of Azkaban* and through his ultra-grim PD James adaptation from 2006, *Children Of Men*, which contained numerous action sequences choreographed and photographed as single unbroken scenes. **DJ**

ADMIT ONE
ONLY

WHAT I LOVE ABOUT MOVIES

FEATURING

RYAN GOSLING

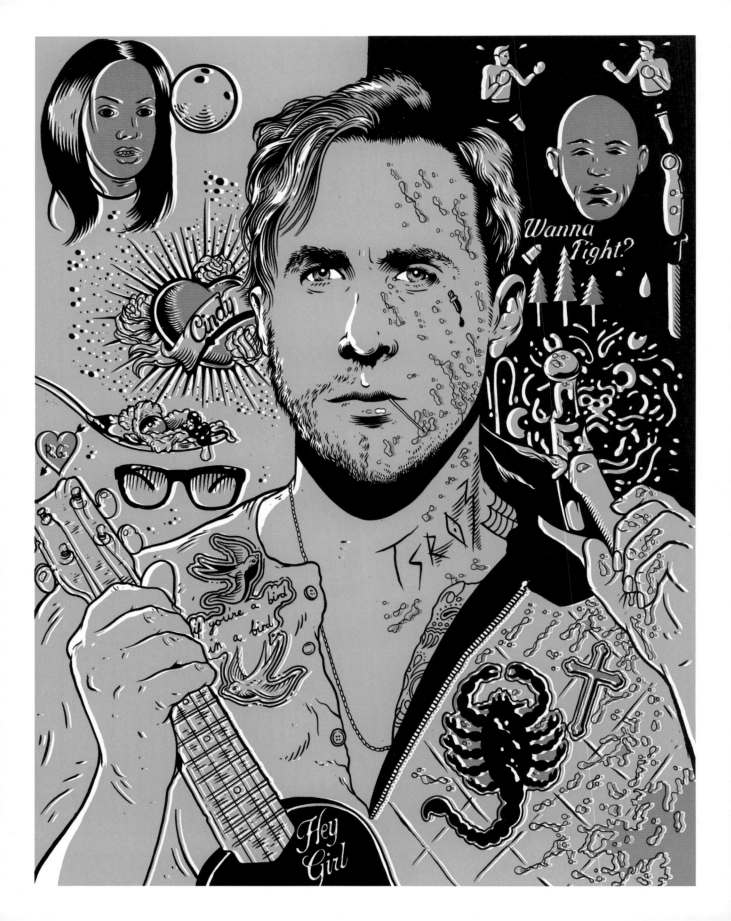

"Well, I think, not to keep harping on the same note, I think... Well, for instance when I was in the fourth grade, maybe even... I forget what year, but it was sometime in junior school that I first saw *First Blood* and it kinda put me under a spell. I believed I was Rambo, and I filled my Fisher-Price Houdini Kit up with steak knives and took it into school and tried throwing them at some of the kids during recess. I didn't hurt anybody, thank God, and I learned my lesson, you know, I'm sorry that I did it... But films have such a powerful effect on me, they always have done. I've tried to control that but I don't think I've ever really managed to. But I don't think I'm alone in recognising that."

Illustration by
TIM MCDONAGH

H e's an internet meme-spawning sensation who earned his first Academy Award nomination before his thirtieth birthday. A former Disney Club Mousketeer who secured a place at Hollywood's top table via a succession of ground-shaking performances. A limelight-shunning heartthrob who cites *First Blood* as a formative influence. The quintessential cool customer with the talent to back it up, Ryan Gosling has had the film world at his feet ever since the 2011 film *Drive* announced the arrival of Hollywood's next major star. Just two years later, however, arguably at the peak of his celebrity, Gosling emabarked on a parallel career as writer/director. Genre-mashing fantasy *How to Catch a Monster* casts Matt Smith and Saoirse Ronan alongside Gosling's former co-stars Christina Hendricks, Eva Mendes and Ben Mendelsohn. It's this mix of ambition, self-awareness and versatility that has endeared Gosling to audiences and critics alike.

Early in his career, Gosling landed the kinds of roles that would be beyond the reach of most rising stars, from a Jewish neo-Nazi in his 2001 breakthrough *The Believer* to a pathological teenage killer in *The United States of Leland* two years later. Part of what sets Gosling apart from his peers is his willingness to roll up his sleeves; he hand-carved a kitchen table for 2004's *The Notebook* and personally refurbished the 1973 Chevy Malibu used in *Drive*. Away from film, Gosling has demonstrated his musical talents as one-half of ethereal indie-rock duo Dead Man's Bones, who released their debut LP in 2009, while quietly establishing himself as a committed social and animal rights campaigner.

Back in front of the lens, Gosling's fruitful collaborations with writer/directors Nicolas Winding Refn (*Drive*, 2013's *Only God Forgives*) and Derek Cianfrance (2010's *Blue Valentine*, 2012's *The Place Beyond the Pines*) have established him as an atypical A-lister who prizes creative harmony over hefty paycheques. Ask Gosling what excites him most about acting and he'll struggle to find the right words. All he can say for sure is that it's the urge to keep creating that motivates him. As long as he maintains that forward-motion, there's no telling what Gosling might achieve. **AW**

WHAT I LOVE ABOUT MOVIES

FEATURING

DARREN ARONOFSKY

"The close-up. It's an overlooked great invention of the 20th century. The fact that one can stare into someone's eyes without being self-conscious is a great gift to all of us. It's why I love cinema."

Illustration by
LUKE DROZD

A quote by director Darren Aronofsky: "If you want to be a filmmaker, the best thing you can bring to the world is your own story." Considering his predilection for grotesque body horror, this could be a rather alarming personal red flag. *Pi* (1998), *Requiem For A Dream* (2000), *The Wrestler* (2008) and *Black Swan* (2010) boast scenes not of the physical slap-bang-wallop that movies routinely dole out as fantasy grist to the mill, but smaller, creepier visual variations on themes of pain and mutilation. Witness Natalie Portman's cuticles peeling back in *Black Swan*, or Jared Leto's yawning, junk-induced flesh hole in *Requiem*. Aronofsky wants to make you wince. He wants to rattle you in your seat. One might compare his tendencies to those of the body horror maestro, David Cronenberg, but Aronofsky refuses to employ irony as an escape route.

Alongside the physical, it's intense psychological suffering that Aronofsky wants to share with the world. Thumping split screens in *Requiem* show the manifold, divergent personal hells the characters have come to occupy. The 'SnorriCam' – a reverse-POV camera attached to an actor's body – is a favoured Aronofsky device. These techniques that aim to latch a viewer directly to in-the-moment sensations extend to heightened sound recording and reliance on composer Clint Mansell. The latter's scores blend hysterical, churning strings with techno breakbeats to convey anxiety and oppression.

Aronofsky didn't discover filmmaking until he was switched on to it by a friend when they were both studying at Harvard. Editing interested him from the beginning and he has always been an assured stylist, using technical flourishes and carefully composed mise-en-scène to reinforce pet themes of fear, threat, obsession and madness. An indie filmmaker willing to fight to fund his projects, 2014's biblical epic *Noah* represents an offbeat decision for him. It uses a mainstream source, and until now he has relished the chance to build up his own worlds from scratch, gradually working through a list of ideas drawn up post-university. 2007's *The Fountain* remains something of an outlier in his small but supple body of work – a gleaming and comparatively serene sci-fi yarn about love, death and the whole bit which starred his then-wife, Rachel Weisz. Nestled in the obscure but heartfelt intergalactic layers are hints of the gentler side to Aronofsky's tales of death, decay and the descent into unyielding insanity. **SMK**

WHAT I LOVE ABOUT MOVIES

FEATURING

RALPH FIENNES

"Well, it's kind of a glib answer, but I feel that movies transport you. A projected image takes you somewhere almost immediately. An image that moves. Aside from saying that I love a great story and a great story being told well, I just love putting on a movie and seeing that first image. I just love it. What's it going to do for me? A photograph – a photograph that moves! – can suddenly find an echo inside you. Then there's your subjective response, and on that is built a face, a character, a story, a moment, a sequence of events. I love the beginning of a film, the first thing I'm being invited to look at. Something just lands inside your soul. The first contact that image has on your inner being. I love that."

Illustration by
THOMAS DANTHONY

▼

There can be no more auspicious start to a garlanded acting career than leap-frogging from a bit-part in British TV detective serial *Prime Suspect* in 1991 to landing one of the topline roles as an SS officer in Steven Spielberg's multi-award winning *Schindler's List* just two years later. This is exactly how things went down for British thespian Ralph Fiennes. A lauded member of the Royal Shakespeare Company who still divides his performing duties between stage, screen and television, Fiennes is an actor who has the uncanny ability for reinvention and excels in roles which, on paper, would appear ill-fitting. Perhaps it's his classical training that led him to roles such as the husky-voiced, bed-ridden archaeologist in Anthony Minghella's luxe literary saga, *The English Patient* from 1996? Or to play Eugene Onegin in his sister Martha's stately adaptation of the nineteenth century Pushkin novel?

But it's the very fact that we think we've pegged who Fiennes is and where his comfort zone lies that make his occasionally eccentric career choices so exciting. One of his greatest performances was as a destitute, extremely fragile mental patient who is released and allowed to fend for himself in a dingy London halfway house in David Cronenberg's intense 2002 psychodrama, *Spider*. The film saw Fiennes dispatching with his broad-shoulder, booming-voiced typecast to (literally) get his hands dirty as a flexible and self-challenging character actor. The surprise that he could suppress his posh drawl enough to convince as a cockney hard-nut in Marin McDonagh's *In Bruges* (2008) was reason enough for celebration. He even began injecting glossy Hollywood behemoths with a dash of class, playing Hades in camp CG runaround, *Clash of the Titans* (2010), and Lord Voldemort from the final two *Harry Potter* movies, a character whose embodiment of unalloyed evil arguably sits on a par with that of Darth Vader.

Not content to merely surprise as a performer (he even exposed his considerable comic chops as a dashing and fruity concierge in Wes Anderson's 2014 film, *The Grand Budapest Hotel*), Fiennes has begun a dual life as a director. His debut feature, *Coriolanus*, from 2011, relocated the Bard's historical tragedy from ancient to modern-day Rome. Two years later he returned and proved himself even more assured behind the tiller as 2013's *The Invisible Woman* offered a quietly intense and scrupulously dramatised study of Charles Dickens' secret mistress, Nelly Ternan. **DJ**

ADMIT ONE
ONLY

WHAT I LOVE ABOUT MOVIES

FEATURING

TERRY GILLIAM

"Very little, these days. Why do I have to keep watching the same movie again and again and again? Okay, so the costumes change, but the explosions look the same, the car chases look the same... I find that movies are becoming repetitive now, the big ones I'm talking about, not the small independent ones where there's still life and hope."

Illustration by
DAN MUMFORD

Terry Gilliam is a wildly imaginative visual concept artist who often favours knocking along overheatedly from one lavish set piece to another over the simple, banal inconvenience of story. But even detractors would concede that the dystopian megalopolis of 1985's *Brazil* is as influential as the future cityscapes of *Metropolis* (1927) and *Blade Runner* (1982), an oppressive system rendered flawlessly from literal architectural top to bottom. And when forced to closely follow others' templates in *Twelve Monkeys* (1995) and *Fear and Loathing in Las Vegas* (1998), Gilliam smoothly inserted his flourishes into a strong narrative rather than making his set stylings the whole story; excess upon excess ishis sporadic, self-imposed cross to bear.

Brazil pitted an imaginative naif against a reflexively repressive bureaucracy, a role its director is seemingly doomed to enact repeatedly. The sole animator and American member of the Monty Python comedy troupe, Gilliam didn't seek out the limelight; in his telling, ill fate necessitated his being thrust into constant self-promotion to defend his work. When appalled Universal executive Sid Sheinberg threw *Brazil* into the vault to linger in distribution purgatory, Gilliam undertook a very public campaign to get his film released, the first of many high-profile production conflicts.

Gilliam's dreamers battle and sometimes precipitate apocalypse, their quests all the more laudably pure for their futility but no less potentially destructive for that. This is perhaps why his many doomed attempts to film Cervantes' 'Don Quixote' feel so apt; like that deluded knight, Gilliam's legend is as much about failure as success. To counter what he contends is an unjust reputation for profligacy and poor production management, Gilliam hired documentary team Keith Fulton and Louis Pepe to follow him on the relatively smooth-going set of *Twelve Monkeys* in case anything went wrong. It was a form of insurance that either backfired or validated him when the same team captured one of his tilts at Quixote falling apart in less than a week. Gilliam didn't precipitate set-destroying floods or cause his star to suffer a production-terminating injury; once again, however, the director was a magnetic martyr for trouble, an image that has now become inseparable from the worlds he's actually realised. **VR**

ADMIT ONE
ONLY

WHAT I LOVE ABOUT MOVIES

FEATURING

CAREY MULLIGAN

▼

"I love escapism more than anything, and I wonder why I don't try harder to be in big fantasy films or Indiana Jones remakes. I love shutting off and being somewhere else."

Illustration by
KELLY THOMPSON

Carey Mulligan is an actor with serious poise. She knows it, and uses it to great effect, allowing the camera pick up on the surface ripples of internalised conflicts, compelling it to return to her until they are released, little by little or in vast, harrowing torrents.

Her break-out role as Jenny in Lone Scherfig's wry adaptation of Lynn Barber's memoir, *An Education* (2009) is a masterclass in pure affectation. The pretence at sophistication of an old-before-her-years schoolgirl swept off her feet by a fast-living older man is her flimsy ticket to adult experience. Only the audience sees the untapped naïvety beneath the oceans of confidence and moxie. Mulligan exploits her brown, deer-in-the-headlamp eyes and elfin, porcelain face to express a vulnerability that stands apart from actorly posturing.

An Education was a career springboard for Mulligan, but it was in 2011 when the girls-school educated, quietly religious actor from Westminster, London landed herself in the big leagues, starring opposite Ryan Gosling in *Drive* and Michael Fassbender in *Shame*. Her role of waifish love interest and weary mother Irene in Nicolas Winding Refn's *Drive* was contained and dignified, the polar opposite to the extrovert, messy Sissy, sister to Fassbender's sex addict Brandon in *Shame*. We first meet her clambering out of the shower naked, before she sings a sultry, slowed-down rendition of 'New York, New York' in a single take. She says that she learned to sing on the hoof.

To win the role of this self-destructive exhibitionist, Mulligan admits she had to beg director Steve McQueen. It was a confession perhaps intended to establish a rawness that eluded an actress whose public profile had been as refined as her numerous turns in period dramas. Her spiky, foul-mouthed folk chanteuse, Jean, in the Coen brothers' *Inside Llewyn Davis* (2013) worked even better with prior knowledge of the more reserved past performances. While it's possible to pose the obvious theory that her external stillness masks a turbulent inner life, a likelier reading is that Mulligan is a curious performer, stirred by damaged characters distant from her own self and smart enough to realise that her professional access to these roles depends upon avoiding typecasting and keeping her private life hidden from public view. **SMK**

ADMIT ONE
ONLY

WHAT I LOVE ABOUT MOVIES

FEATURING

STEVEN SODERBERGH

"It's an immersion that I think is unique. In the summer of 1975, I was 12 and I saw *Jaws*. It freaked me out so completely it was almost like a civil claims court: 'I need to know more about who did this to me.' A year later, I got my hands on a camera. And the question was then, 'Well, can I do this to people?' And that's been the question I've been answering in one form or another for the past 32 years."

Illustration by

SAMUEL ROGERS

I t was the numbers that got him in the end. In April of 2013, American director Steven Soderbergh took to the stage at the 56th San Francisco International Film Festival to deliver a keynote speech on the state of cinema. Among the many pearls of wisdom gathered during 20 years at the filmmaking vanguard ("Movies are something you watch, cinema is something you make"), Soderbergh outlined his dissatisfaction with the backwards mechanics of "the industry" as a way to bolster his decision to bid adieu to filmmaking in order to explore alternate artistic avenues, most notably TV and painting.

Even though he's a filmmaker who'll likely be eulogised for titles such as the swingin'neo-Rat Pack "Ocean's" trilogy, his 1989 Palme d'Or-winning debut feature *sex, lies and videotape*, or 2012's unlikely box office behemoth, *Magic Mike*, it's one of his lesser-known projects that comes closest to defining his motivations as an artist. 1996's *Schizopolis* was Soderbergh's barmy, coolly-cynical ode to one of his heroes, British filmmaker Richard Lester. Though an ample synopsis of this madcap experimental work-out would likely fill this entire volume, the film's central motifs of warring identities and arch-deconstruction of generic movie gestures and etiquettes speaks of Soderbergh's own peculiar status within the Hollywood firmament.

Here was a sensitive and intuitive filmmaker adapting to harsh corporate strictures, dividing his time between big projects which made money and won awards (*Traffic* and *Erin Brokovich*, both from 2000) and smaller, more experimentally-inclined projects which challenged the norms of the medium both in front of and behind the camera (2005's *Bubble*, 2008's *The Girlfriend Experience*, 2002's *Full Frontal*, the brilliant, two-part *Che* from 2008). In the late flurry of activity that preceded his pre-announced retirement, Soderbergh – as if to bite a thumb at the industry he was so ambivalent towards – delivered a series of stunning, un-ironic genre features that act as a showcase for his effortless directorial mastery. *Haywire* (2011) placed stunt-woman Gina Carano front-and-centre in a martial arts spy caper that trumps just about every Bond movie ever made, *Contagion* from the same year paid icky lip service to the star-powered '70s disaster movie, while *Side Effects* (2013) expertly rehoused Hitchcock's *Psycho* (1960) in the pharma-afflicted '00s. **DJ**

ADMIT ONE
ONLY

WHAT I LOVE ABOUT MOVIES

FEATURING

STEVE MCQUEEN

"It can be one of the best experiences you can have. You know, I've been in cinemas and I've been sitting down and I've looked at things in front of me and been totally moved. If you can be moved by a movie, if a movie stirs you, gives you goose pimples, makes you feel different when you walk outside onto the street and see daylight, that's something unique. There was a wonderful old cinema called the Lumière, it was underground, like a whale's stomach. You used to go down those stairs and into this cave and the movie would finish and you'd climb the stairs into the light and noise of the street... That is an amazing thing to me, that feeling of pure inspiration. It's just magic. Now it's a fucking gym. That's modern life."

Illustration by

TELEGRAMME

▼

The humanism of Steve McQueen comes from a place that at first glance seems lacking in basic humanity. Each of his three films focus on isolated and trapped men, one in prison (2008's *Hunger*), one in addiction (2011's *Shame*) and one in slavery (2013's *12 Years a Slave*). He tells each of these stories in minute close-up, ensuring the specifics of each individual's suffering are writ large across the screen. And this is the nature of Steve McQueen's humanism. He believes that we have a responsibility to face up fully and unflinchingly to the worst in our world; that it's within our capabilities.

Before he was a director, Steve McQueen was an artist, who won the Turner prize and was given an OBE in 2002. (A CBE followed in 2011.) Such establishment recognition represented a head-spinning turnaround from boyhood days at Drayton Manor High School in London where he encountered institutional racism and was put in a class for students thought best-suited to a career in manual labour. If McQueen's work is now full of social and political bite, then maybe it's because he himself has been bitten.

He knows his enemies but also his friends, drawing on the skills of regular collaborators. Cinematographer Sean Bobbit and actor Michael Fassbender have worked on each of his three films. With the help of Bobbitt, McQueen has continued to make an arresting visual impression. Agonising long takes stand out in his work: an anguished night-time job through the New York streets in *Shame*; a sun-lit rural day with a man hanging from a noose in *12 Years A Slave*. Scenes like these outlast most in contemporary cinema, both in time and in the memory. An artist's awareness of how a single image can sear itself onto the mind has stayed with McQueen.

Notoriously short-tempered with questions or individuals he believes are stupid or thoughtless, McQueen in life and in work is a man who doesn't suffer fools gladly. While this may sometimes sting, the verbal and cinematic lashes he dispenses are all in the name of directing our attention to stories of the utmost importance. **SMK**

ADMIT ONE
ONLY

WHAT I LOVE ABOUT MOVIES

FEATURING

TIM BURTON

"Movies for me are therapeutic. I've always thought films, like fairy tales, explore concepts such as life and death in a safe way. They help you learn how to cope and find your place in the world. Characters played by the likes of Vincent Price and Christopher Lee, or monsters such as Frankenstein and the Creature from the Black Lagoon were always something I could emotionally relate to. Similarly, making movies is basically an expensive form of therapy."

Illustration by

BRADLEY JAY

Tim Burton doesn't make films so much as build cascading monuments to trash auteurs, eccentric oddballs and superannuated "art" which, to many eyes, would barely be worthy of that hallowed moniker. With regular access to studio millions, Burton's cinema translates as a sweetly earnest attempt to enshrine his veritably kitsch tastes within the type of grand, high-production-value epics that his forebears could barely have imagined. 1994's *Ed Wood*, for example, captures the creative life of the infamous "worst filmmaker of all time", photographing a gorgeously up-lit '50s Hollywood in luminescent monochrome and starring one of the world's most famous men, Johnny Depp. Though a box-office failure on its release, the film works as a blueprint for Burton's cinema, arguing that, yes, bad artists are often oblivious to their creative shortcomings, but that there's also untapped and untenable beauty to be found in these "maudit" works of personal wonder.

Burton kicked off his filmmaking career in 1984 with a masterpiece in the form of the rollicking, medium-length reanimation fantasy, *Frankenweenie*, which was deemed "too scary" by Disney backers and was duly shelved. (Ironically, he would go on to produce a feature-length stop-motion remake of the film for the same company 28 years later.) TV comedy star Pee-Wee Herman (played by Paul Reubens) yomped to the big screen with the help of Burton's keen eye for gaudy comedy, and 1985's *Pee-Wee's Big Adventure* went on to become one of the strangest box-office hits of all time. It was after this that the on-the-rise director began an unimpeachable run from 1988's *Beetlejuice* through to 1996's undervalued *Mars Attacks!*, occasionally adapting his talents as a high-end fabulist for mass consumption (1989's *Batman*, 1992's *Batman Returns*).

It's hard to know whether we're always seeing Burton's pure, unvarnished vision, or one tainted by corporate demands as he often works within the upper echelons of the studio system. It makes him something of a tragic figure, a man who is forced to deliver idiosyncrasy by stealth. The "real" Burton can be seen in such films as his splatter take on the Sondheim musical, *Sweeney Todd: The Demon Barber of Fleet Street* (2007), or even his peculiarly melancholic and acidly funny refit of '60s gothic soap opera, *Dark Shadows* (2012). One theme unites all of his films – and perhaps hints at an element of doleful autobiography: an attraction to maverick or maligned outsiders attempting to find meaning and acceptance behind the chintzy curtain of cosy, hum-drum normality. **DJ**

ADMIT ONE
ONLY

WHAT I LOVE ABOUT MOVIES

• FEATURING •

RIAN JOHNSON

"Wow. Er... I feel like movies have been...
Movies are my earliest memory of storytelling.
The earliest memories I have of being
transported by a story are of watching movies
and that's just carried through the rest of
my life. And... I think there's nothing more
powerful to me than sitting in a theatre and,
you know... God, this is so clichéd I feel like I'm
on an interstitial Oscars broadcast. 'There's
nothing better than being transported by film!'
But there is nothing more powerful than being
transported by film, so there you go."

Illustration by

MAT PRINGLE

Rian Johnson is a genre-recombining classicist whose films operate with a high degree of self-awareness. He is committed to executing satisfying renditions of micro-genre pastiches without losing his ever-inventive vocabulary or eye for high gloss. Critic Raymond Durgnat proposed that conceiving of distinct genres as sets of coherent checklists ignored the possibility for the comedy, horror, thriller et al to assimilate parts that seemingly don't belong. "Some films are pure westerns," he observed, "but many films are hybrids, just as most dogs are mongrels." So it is with Johnson's films, whose starting reference points draw in seemingly disparate or incongruous elements.

In 2005 feature debut *Brick*, Johnson proposed that an American high school — a site of fast-burn glory for some, a torturous testing ground for others — was the logical lawless setting for a modern noir enacted by dangerous women and many-times-burned men. Characters have names like "Tugger" and "The Brain," their Chandler-esque speech is devoted to verbal play for its own sake. Against the odds, Johnson doesn't get bogged down in admiring his own dexterity. *Brick* is the story of a young man whose adroitness at his self-imposed private investigator tasks can't mask a deep well of crippling emotional pain, as the movie itself makes a last-minute shift from crisp entertainment to gut-punch devastation.

With 2008's *The Brothers Bloom*, Johnson attempted the risky micro-genre project of making his very own Wes Anderson film. A crime comedy gloss on *The Royal Tenenbaums*, *Bloom* comes complete with unflappable Ricky Jay narration and a heroine whose Max Fischer-esque interests encompass kung fu and juggling. An even trickier balancing act than *Brick*, *Bloom* similarly bides its sprightly time until a self-sacrificing ending. Ditto *Looper* (2012), in which Johnson turned his attention to comparatively big-budget sci-fi, merging a Bruce Willis action film with a bad seed drama; predictably, it ends in the last place you would have anticipated at the outset. The surface-level entertainment always gives way to a climactic emotional breakdown, though Johnson has also displayed adaptive adeptness at directing from others' templates on three episodes of TV's *Breaking Bad*. **VR**

WHAT I LOVE ABOUT MOVIES

• FEATURING •

MICHAEL FASSBENDER

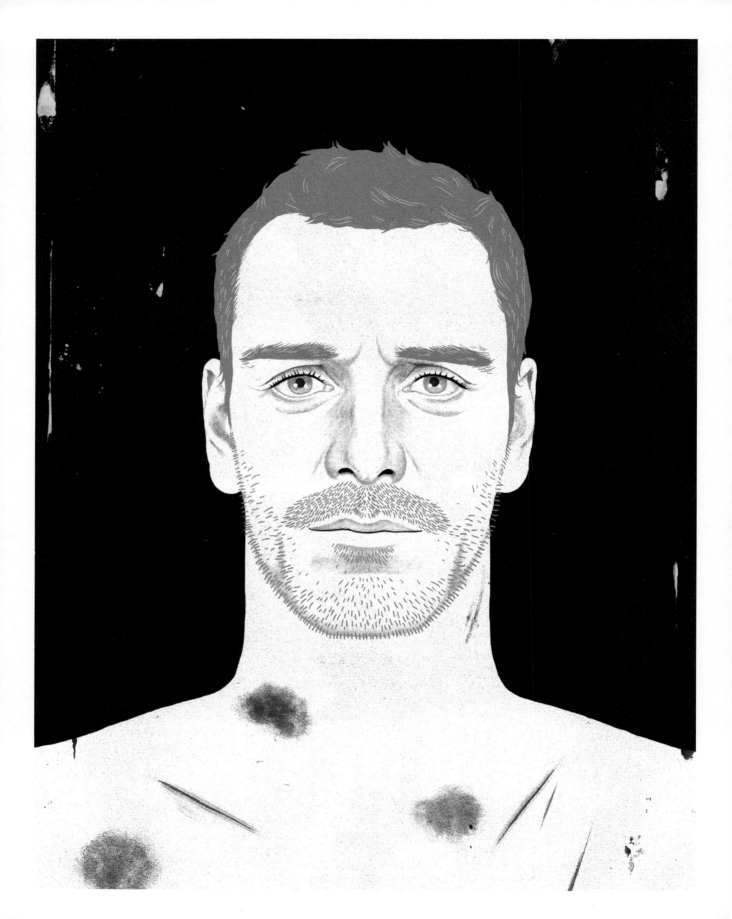

"I suppose going right back to when they really, sort of, struck home... It's that thing of, you know, we're trying to figure out our place in the world and what it's all about, and 'where do we fit it?', and 'do we fit in?' and... I think movies are a way to, sort of, reflect other people's affectations or positions or how they are trying to, sort of, deal with things. And when you see something it's just like 'I'm not alone.' Or I like the experience of just escaping into another world for an hour-and-a-half and going on that journey and being allowed to be taken somewhere else... I've always found that a very expressive form of art and, sort of, one that I could relate to from teenage years onwards."

Illustration by
PAUL X. JOHNSON

From crash-dieting for his portrayal of an emaciated prisoner in *Hunger* (2007) to going full frontal in *Shame* (2011), Michael Fassbender has always relished exploring the ingrained physicality of his craft. Behind the scenes, the Irish-German actor is known as a stickler for scripting, reportedly poring over screenplays up to 300 times before stepping foot on set. In conversation, he gives the impression of being someone who's had to graft hard to get ahead and will continue to do so for the sake of a good story. And yet, there is nothing egotistical or pretentious about Fassbender (though anyone who's seen Lenny Abrahamson's *Frank* (2014) might wish to argue the case for Fassbender's bigheadedness).

With his classy-cool demeanour and chiselled good looks, Fassbender is equal parts Laurence Olivier and Richard Burton. A regular of franchise behemoths such as *X-Men: First Class* (2011) and *Prometheus* (2012) in recent years, he appears more at home in intimate period pieces like *Jane Eyre* (2011), *A Dangerous Method* (2011) and *12 Years a Slave* (2013). The latter marked Fassbender's third film with British director Steve McQueen (following *Hunger* and *Shame*), a fruitful union that turned Fassbender into a permanent fixture on the awards circuit. Fassbender is keen to build on the relationship, having spoken at length about becoming, he hopes, the De Niro to McQueen's Scorsese.

In between earning an early career calling card in Steven Spielberg and Tom Hanks' 2001 World War Two mini-series, *Band of Brothers*, and making his feature debut as a young Spartan warrior in Zack Snyder's 2006 green screen epic, *300*, Fassbender spent years doing the rounds in various British television dramas. Success didn't come easy. But if it took Fassbender a long time to arrive, he certainly seized his moment and his stock now could hardly be higher. Even so, it's telling that he hasn't forgotten his humble beginnings — he's based not in Los Angeles but unglamorous east London — nor the people who made him. It's no coincidence that Fassbender has been rewarded generously for his work-ethic and loyalty. **AW**

WHAT I LOVE ABOUT MOVIES

FEATURING

NICOLAS WINDING REFN

"What do I love about movies? Um... I'm a product of cinema. Like Hans Christian Andersen from my own country... we try different artforms and fail miserably until we find what works for us. He found fairy tales, I found cinema. What's great about it is it's a great massive construction of emotions that you can release to the public. Success is measured in how people diversely react to what you do, because the line between love and hate is when there's a sense of penetration."

Illustration by
WILL HAYWOOD

At the 2011 Cannes Film Festival, Lars von Trier, Denmark's most famous living filmmaker, was declared "persona non-grata" following Nazi-related digressions made during the press conference for his film *Melancholia*. To the world press corps, this was earthshaking news. With von Trier seemingly out of the frame, who would fill the great provocateur's sizeable shoes? Step forward Nicolas Winding Refn, who announced himself with tyre-screeching aplomb two days later with his candy-hued auto-thriller, *Drive*. Long considered the natural heir to his mischievous countryman, Refn left the French Riviera that summer with the Best Director award in hand and critical acclaim ringing in his ears. On stage, he thanked his mother.

Refn's return to Cannes two years later proved more divisive. His hypnotic Bangkok-set fever-dream, *Only God Forgives*, again starred Ryan Gosling but premiered to mixed reviews. Despite this, it cemented Refn's growing reputation as a bold director with a clear personal vision who relishes eliciting a strong visceral response from audiences. Refn's propensity for orchestrating set pieces whose ultra-violence is sometimes excruciating makes him both an exciting and potentially corruptive force. Yet there is much more to Refn's work than cheap thrills and sex appeal.

Now in his mid-forties, Refn has matured considerably from the young punk director who lit up the mean streets of Copenhagen with his searing 1996 debut, *Pusher*, a film which earnt him lofty comparisons to a young Scorsese. His distinctive grasp of the visual language of cinema has become more refined, and today there are those who would argue that Refn belongs in the same class as the world's most revered auteurs. If there's one thing *Only God Forgives* proved above all else, however, it's that Refn hasn't mellowed with age. He remains a maverick, a deviant – especially by Hollywood's standards. Indeed, Refn's bold decision to turn his back on Tinseltown following the success of *Drive* and instead commit to less commercially attractive projects — including *Only God Forgives* and a TV revival of *Barbarella* — was perceived as a statement of devious intent. It most probably was. **AW**

WHAT I LOVE ABOUT MOVIES

FEATURING

WALTER MURCH

"Well, it's unique in artistry when you compare it to sculpture or painting or dance, because you can think of it as a theatre of thought. It's the first time we've been able to choreograph human thought and make it understandable and watch people think on screen in motion. Obviously photographs can do this and paintings can capture a moment, and theatre does it to a certain extent, but it all happens through language. Music, you can say, is thought and emotion in a very abstract sense. But here we're actually looking at specific human beings, watching them think and getting a huge kick out of that, because in life that's mostly what we do. Film is the artistic manipulation of that same idea."

No less than Francis Ford Coppola, George Lucas and other '70s film-school brats, Walter Murch is still mythologised as a disruptive Hollywood game-changer. He's probably the only sound designer that general film enthusiasts speak of in hushed, reverential tones, fittingly since that particular designation is accepted as his linguistic invention. Because of the sometimes showy, literally multi-layered brilliance of his work designing the soundscapes of *American Graffiti* (1973), *Apocalypse Now* (1979) and *The Godfather* trilogy (1972, 1974, 1990), Murch's wackiest pronouncements are given due consideration.

Take, for example, his idea that foley re-recording should never be done by using the actual object whose sound needs to be recaptured. Instead, a different object should be found to produce the sound needed. Like a Renaissance microcosm constructor, Murch understands all of a movie's properties as working on an analogical basis, representing both the literal thing being contemplated and a suggestive enrichment of same. In famously eliding the whooshing of a hotel room's ceiling fan with the rotation of helicopter blades in *Apocalypse Now*, Murch succinctly expressed his belief that the smallest details can link different worlds.

A conspicuously eccentric polymath, Murch's leisure time pursuits include translating the work of controversial Italian writer Curzio Malaparte and speaking extensively on his philosophy of cinema. Don't mistake his adventurous spirit for a lack of pragmatism or technical woolly-headedness: an early adopter and innovator, *The English Patient* (1996) earned him the first Oscar for editing on an electronic system. Murch's prodigious technical skills have sometimes left him mired in hack-for-hire work, salvaging the unsavable, putting in editorial time on doomed projects like Charles Shyer's *I Love Trouble* (1994) or Joe Johnston's ill-starred remake of *The Wolfman* (2010).

Spare a thought for his sole feature directorial credit, 1985's grand curiosity *Return To Oz*. That the film introduced cult star Fairuza Balk to unsuspecting child audiences is the least of its accomplishments, in which only Dorothy can save rubble-strewn Oz. Its electroshock opening sets the stage for the ingeniously terrifying image of a villainous queen wandering a gallery of dismembered heads in search of a suitable one to wear for the day. Murch's eclectic gallery of unnerving imagery terrified children and angered parents, ensuring stand-alone cult immortality. **VR**

WHAT I LOVE ABOUT MOVIES

FEATURING

JOSEPH GORDON-LEVITT

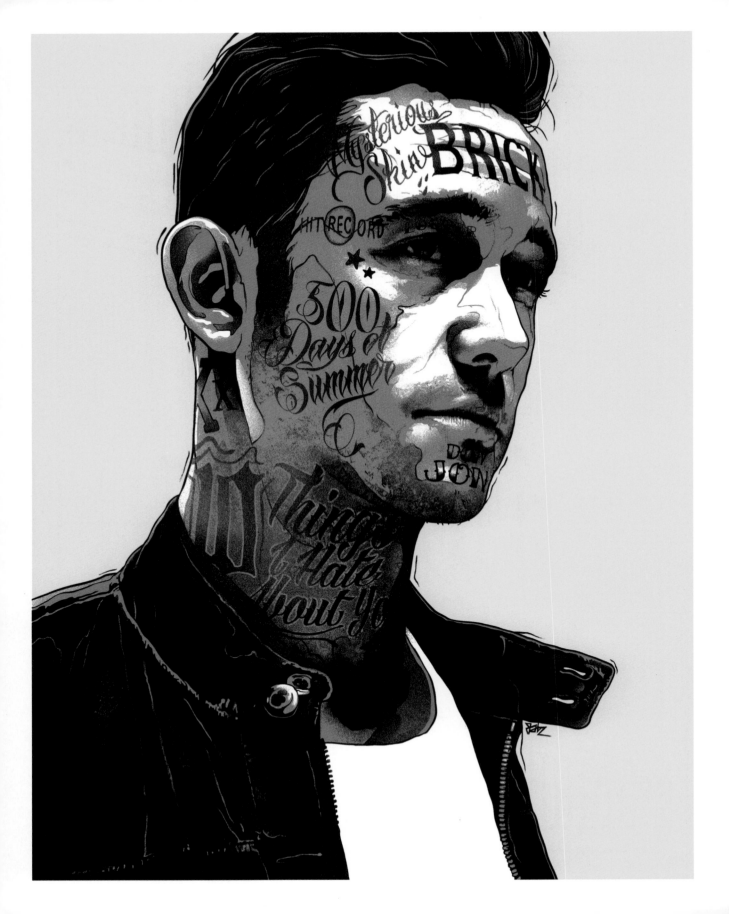

"What do I love about movies?
I love being able to see the world from someone else's perspective. We spend our whole lives inside our own head and getting to see what it looks like — or at least an estimation or abstraction of what it looks like — from someone else's point of view, that's beautiful. That's I guess part of what makes us uniquely human, is our ability to do that."

Illustration by
GABZ

Eerily, Joseph Gordon-Levitt's face has scarcely aged since his child star days on whipsmart sci-fi sitcom, *3rd Rock from the Sun* (1996-2001). Now, Levitt is all grown up in terms of his ambitions as a performer and, lately, a writer/director. In 2005, along with brother Dan, he also founded web-based production company hitRECord. At its point of inception, it was a way for JGL – who had just cleared his schedule by dropping out of Columbia University – to get instant feedback on his work, but the operation has since snowballed into a professional duty. It was used to fund *Don Jon*, Gordon-Levitt's inaugural directorial effort from 2013, about a young man's blind obsession with meaningless sex.

HitRECord attained extra significance due to Dan's untimely death in 2010. As it has flourished, Levitt has embraced the possibilities offered by being a respected online personality. Short films, live performances and a TV show have come out of hitRECord's creative community and all boast Gordon-Levitt at their forefront. Renaissance man and entrepreneur he may be, but straight-up acting remains the main source of his fame. This is curious because, despite his talent and natural presence, JGL has arguably yet to find his definitive screen role.

Embodying the handsome, good-humoured everyman, he has cruised through his share of superior teen flicks. Yet, unlike so much disposable multiplex-fodder, *10 Things I Hate About You* (1999) and *(500) Days of Summer* (2009) have endured in the public imagination. The former, an adaptation of Shakespeare's *The Taming of the Shrew*, has become a countercultural classic, slotting neatly alongside John Hughes' bratpack flicks in teen-movie-marathon all-nighters. He occasionally explores more haunted and haunting characters, notably an abuse-victim-turned-gay-hustler in Greg Araki's 2004 feature, *Mysterious Skin*, and a hard-bitten high-school gumshoe in Rian Johnson's *Brick* (2005). In these roles, his tendencies towards easy expressiveness are pared back to something quieter and tauter. He is reaching for a severity that reared its head in Johnson's time-travelling action thriller *Looper* (2012) and, to a certain extent, *Don Jon*. It sits oddly with the nice, ambitious man incapable of unpleasantness in an interview and who wears odd socks as a cryptic memorial to his brother. **SMK**

WHAT I LOVE ABOUT MOVIES

• FEATURING •

RICHARD LINKLATER

"Wow. That's such a big question. I think fundamentally what I love about movies is the parallel reality of them. They're a more selective, more attuned and more neatly edited version of life itself. It's improved life. I don't know, man, you put a guy on the spot like this... It's just life. That's all I can say."

Illustration by

NICHOLAS JOHN FRITH

▼

There is a tendency for film dialogue to sound exactly like film dialogue – human speech that's been cleaved and contrived to fit the purposes of cosy dramatic arcs. Of his manifold talents as a filmmaker – one of America's finest, without doubt – Texan Richard Linklater has perfected a style of cinematic storytelling which accounts for the abstract messiness of how people talk to one another. Verbalised thoughts cascade and buffet and break off and sometimes even locate transcendence. In the brilliant opening scene to his seminal 1991 breakthrough feature *Slacker*, Linklater himself appears playing a winsome deadbeat, offering a deep textural analysis of his own dreams which segues gently into some sincerely articulated postulations on chaos theory.

Talk is never cheap in a Linklater movie, its nuance carrying the weight of future contentment in his *Before* films, clarifying the vagaries of dream logic in his ambling RotoScoped essay, *Waking Life*, and used to inflict unimaginable pain in his single-setting three-hander, *Tape*. His professed love of movies such as Jean Eustache's *The Mother and the Whore* as well as the works of French master Eric Rohmer suggest that Linklater's way with film dialogue – and not merely writing it, but filming it – finds its lineage in some of the great "talky" movies of all time.

Formal innovation abounds within Linklater's sparkling and diverse film oeuvre, from the use of idiosyncratic animation techniques in films like 2006's *A Scanner Darkly*, mixing fiction and documentary in 2012's viscously funny *Bernie* (which gifted actor Jack Black with a peach of a role) and even creating a lilting rite of passage drama that was filmed with the same actors over 12 consecutive years in 2014's masterful *Boyhood*. His various attempts to court mainstream attention have ranged from the strong (2003's *School of Rock*) to the likably mediocre (1995's *The Newton Boys*, 2005's *The Bad News Bears*), though he's clearly a filmmaker more at home when the perfume of experimentation is allowed to linger in the air. His cinephile credentials are also second to none, having founded the Austin Film Society in order to bring obscure art cinema to the Deep South in 1985, and remaining its chairman to this very day. **DJ**

WHAT I LOVE ABOUT MOVIES

FEATURING

JOANNA HOGG

"I've got very eclectic taste in films. I enjoy laughing. I've been watching some Buster Keaton. That's been very enjoyable. When I was about 11 or 12 I started to become interested in films. I was a big fan of Hollywood musicals, particularly Gene Kelly because I like tap-dancing. My imagination was captured by musicals. The Powell and Pressburger film *The Red Shoes* had a powerful effect on me because I was very interested in reading fairy tales. Somehow fairy tales, particularly [*those by the*] Brothers Grimm and Hans Christian Andersen, and films were very connected in my young mind at that time. Somehow films are a container for dreams and that's something I feel that I'm connecting more with again, having had a number of years when I didn't feel that I managed to marry my interest in fairy tales and dreams with my filmmaking but that's coming back. I find that very exciting. Film is somewhere you can escape to with your imagination, where you can engage your imagination so you're both watching a creation and creating it for yourself at the same time."

Illustration by
ESSY MAY

W hat do we think about when we think about British cinema? Kitchen sinks? Grubby urchins high-tailing it down cobbled northern streets? Cockney wide-boys in sharp suits brandishing phallic shooters in London's East End? Joanna Hogg is a British filmmaker whose work can be decoded as an unmistakable (and often slyly unflattering) commentary on British character and social habits. At the same time, she choses to look towards Europe, Asia and Russia as influences for her rarified formal adventures.

An early acolyte of Derek Jarman and a stalwart of British television drama, Hogg directed her first feature in 2007. *Unrelated* is a bitterly funny and scathing survey of bourgeois Brits abroad and the subtle tensions of age, friendship and jealousy among a broad and emotionally ineffectual family grouping. Hogg's mode is one of mordant, bleak naturalism, where dialogue rarely dictates the shape of a scene; instead, awkward silences often articulate an insidious sense of frustration and depression. Her second feature, *Archipelago* (2010), saw Hogg refine rather than expand her chosen cinematic voice, drafting in once more the talents of her greatest discovery, Tom Hiddleston, as a member of yet another family harbouring a multitude of simmering resentments. The film's most memorable scene involves a disastrous visit to a restaurant where personalities clash like the waves breaking on the coastal backdrop. It verified Hogg's adeptness at combining the serious psychological profiling of a family in the process of gradual disintegration with an appropriately mischievous and dark sense of humour.

Hogg's 2013 film, *Exhibition*, moved her cinematic touchstones more prominently to the fore, with references to Jacques Tati, Stanley Kubrick and Andrei Tarkovksy skilfully woven into a story of an artistic power couple who have mysteriously chosen to move out of their plush modernist stack. When not writing and directing feature films, Hogg and filmmaker Adam Roberts run a repertory screening society, named A Nos Amours after the 1983 Maurice Pialat film. With a remit to programme rare and obscure arthouse titles and for their exhibition to be strictly from celluloid, the pair have managed to show films such as Fred Kelemen's 1997 slow-cinema opus, *Frost*, and an entire retrospective of work by Belgian master, Chantal Akerman. **DJ**

ADMIT ONE
ONLY

WHAT I LOVE ABOUT MOVIES

FEATURING

THE COEN BROTHERS

"*Joel:* Ehhh... [*pause*]
Ethan: Lunch!
Joel: Lunch is a good answer. I dunno. It's the business we've chosen. You make certain decisions in your life and you either learn to love it or, y'know... So we've learned to love it.
Ethan: Also lunch, you don't have to pay for it. They can't get it back later. Everything else they can get back. But not lunch. Those motherfuckers."

▼

Are there any other living directors responsible for such a bounty of beloved, canonical movies? Naysayers accuse the Coens of lacking in sincerity, though their oeuvre is so pointedly rich and varied that it is hard to comprehend the substance in any kind of blanket dismissal. Perhaps this criticism is born of the brothers' proclivity for making films which focus on (often self-engineered) human failure and a belief that any affront to basic morality will rarely go unpunished. Dan Hedaya's jealous husband in the Coens' stupendous 1984 debut, *Blood Simple*, suffers the blow-back of a scheme to catch his wife (Frances McDormand) in the act with another man (John Getz). For each of the characters, the inexorable mechanics of blind justice grind them into a slurry of madness and violence.

While tainted patsies are liberally littered across the Coens' cinematic upland (think Ed Crane in *The Man Who Wasn't There* from 2001, Jerry Lundegaard in 1996's *Fargo* or the title character in 1995's *Barton Fink*), the writer-director-producer twosome have even started to toy with auto-reflexive films which cheekily question the very nature of divine retribution. In *A Serious Man* (2009), a Jewish maths scholar finds that his life is swiftly and brutally falling apart for reasons beyond his comprehension, almost as if he's been singled out for some variant of Job-style spiritual flagellation. *Inside Llewyn Davis* (2013), a bittersweet musical fable about a flailing New York folk troubadour, also poses acute questions about how we define professional success and failure in a world seemingly driven by incomprehensible forces.

Two of their most notable films were adapted from existing sources: 2007's sand-blasted, existential chase thriller, *No Country For Old Men*, was based on a novel by Cormac McCarthy and won the Coens both Best Picture and Best Director Oscars; *O Brother, Where Art Thou?* (2000), a Bluegrass picaresque starring George Clooney, John Turturro and Tim Blake Nelson as escaped members of an all-singing chain gang, drew ironic inspiration from Homer's 'The Odyssey'. Yet they have claimed in interviews that they seldom make movies that are straight adaptations, instead opting to infuse a range of film and literature and fondly purloining lone elements and ideas on which to build their magnificent movies. **DJ**

ILLUSTRATION CREDITS

FRANCIS FORD COPPOLA
BY WE BUY YOUR KIDS
wbyk.com.au
Interview by Matt Bochenski

SIMON PEGG
BY MISS LOTION
misslotion.com
Interview by Tom Seymour

KRISTEN STEWART
BY RIK LEE
jackywinter.com/artists/rik-lee
Interview by Adam Woodward

CLAIRE DENIS
BY MISS LED
missled.co.uk
Interview by David Jenkins

MILA KUNIS
BY BEC WINNEL
becwinnel.com
Interview by Matt Bochenski

ALEXANDER PAYNE
BY PAUL BLOW
paulblow.com
Interview by Adam Woodward

JAKE GYLLENHAAL
BY ADAM CRUFT
adamcruft.com
Interview by David Jenkins

OLIVIER ASSAYAS
KAROLIN SCHNOOR
karolinschnoor.co.uk
Interview by Matt Bochenski

DANIEL RADCLIFFE
BY SAM DUNN
sam-dunn.com
Interview by Tom Seymour

PEDRO ALMODÓVAR
BY ALEC DOHERTY
alecdoherty.com
Interview by Adam Woodward

JUDE LAW
BY MARIO ZUCCA
mariozucca.com
Interview by Adam Woodward

DANNY BOYLE
BY STEVEN WILSON
stevenwilsonstudio.com
Interview by Jonathan Crocker

RICHARD AYOADE
BY OIVIND HOVLAND
oivindhovland.com
Interview by Adam Woodward

SPIKE JONZE
BY CHRIS DELORENZO
chrisdelorenzo.com
Interview by Sophie Monks Kaufman

VIGGO MORTENSEN
BY LUKE BROOKES
lukebrookesillustration.co.uk
Interview by Matt Bochenski

QUENTIN TARANTINO
BY I LOVE DUST
ilovedust.com
Interview by David Jenkins

HELEN MIRREN
BY GRACE HELMER
gracehelmer.co.uk
Interview by Adam Woodward

JULIETTE BINOCHE
BY KAREENA ZEREFOS
www.kareenazerefos.com
Interview by Adam Woodward

KELLY REICHARDT
BY MONTSE BERNAL
cargocollective.com/montsebernal
Interview by Adam Woodward

JIA ZHANG-KE
BY MOOSE & YETI
mooseandyeti.com
Interview by Elaine Chow

HARMONY KORINE
BY DILRAJ MANN
puckcollective.co.uk/dilraj-mann
Interview by Adam Woodward

JOHN HURT
BY RUPERT SMISSEN
rupertsmissen.co.uk
Interview by David Jenkins

MICHEL GONDRY
BY ELIOT WYATT
cargocollective.com/eliotwyatt
Interview by David Jenkins

CASEY AFFLECK
BY OLIVER STAFFORD
oliverstafford.co.uk
Interview by Adam Woodward

WES ANDERSON
BY ANDREW FAIRCLOUGH
kindredstudio.net
Interview by David Jenkins

MIA WASIKOWSKA
BY ELEANOR TAYLOR
eleanortaylor.co.uk
Interview by Sophie Monks Kaufman

WILLIAM FRIEDKIN
BY HEDOF
hedof.com
Interview by Tom Seymour

TSAI MING-LIANG
BY JENSINE ECKWALL
jensineeckwall.com
Interview by David Jenkins

PHILIP SEYMOUR HOFFMAN
BY RAID71
raid71.com
Interview by Adam Woodward

SHANE CARRUTH
BY DIEGO PATIÑO
diegopatino.com
Interview by Adam Woodward

TOM HARDY
BY JAMES WILSON
jameswilsonillustration.com
Interview by Adam Woodward

TERENCE DAVIES
BY SAM PASH
sampashillustration.com
Interview by Adam Woodward

PARK CHAN-WOOK
BY ELENA GUMENIUK
puckcollective.com/elena-gumeniuk
Interview by David Jenkins

ALFONSO CUARON
BY ZORAN NOVA
cargocollective.com/zorannova
Interview by Mark Salisbury

RYAN GOSLING
BY TIM MCDONAGH
mcdonaghillustration.com
Interview by Adam Woodward

DARREN ARONOFSKY
BY LUKE DROZD
lukedrozd.com
Interview by Matt Bochenski

RALPH FIENNES
BY THOMAS DANTHONY
thomasdanthony.com
Interview by David Jenkins

TERRY GILLIAM
BY DAN MUMFORD
dan-mumford.com
Interview by Matt Thrift

CAREY MULLIGAN
BY KELLY THOMPSON
kellythompson.co.nz
Interview by Matt Bochenski

STEVEN SODERBERGH
BY SAMUEL ROGERS
samuelesquire.com
Interview by Matt Bochenski

STEVE MCQUEEN
BY TELEGRAMME
telegramme.co.uk
Interview by Adam Woodward

TIM BURTON
BY BRADLEY JAY
bradleyjay.co.uk
Interview by Mark Salisbury

RIAN JOHNSON
BY MAT PRINGLE
matpringle.co.uk
Interview by Adam Woodward

MICHAEL FASSBENDER
BY PAUL X. JOHNSON
paulxjohnson.com
Interview by Adam Woodward

NICOLAS WINDING REFN
BY WILL HAYWOOD
willhaywood.com
Interview by Adam Woodward

WALTER MURCH
BY BORIS PELCER
borispelcer.com
Interview by Kingsley Marshall

JOSEPH GORDON-LEVITT
BY GABZ
iamgabz.com
Interview by Adam Woodward

RICHARD LINKLATER
BY NICHOLAS JOHN FRITH
nicholasjohnfrith.com
Interview by Adam Woodward

JOANNA HOGG
BY ESSY MAY
stemagency.com/illustrator/essymay
Interview by Sophie Monks Kaufman

THE COEN BROTHERS
BY MUTI
studiomuti.co.za
Interview by David Jenkins

ENDS

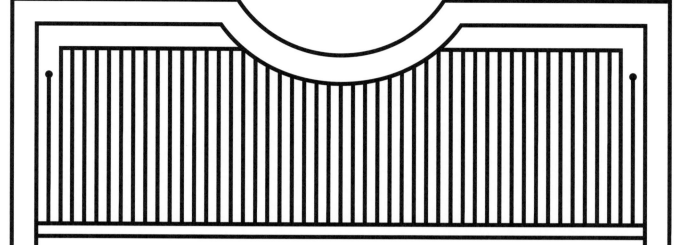

WORDS, PICTURES, THANKS...

To Walter Donohue at Faber and Ed Wilson at Johnson and Alcock for their overwhelming surfeit of sage advice, top cinephile banter and for allowing this thing to happen. To Vince Medieros and Wendy Klerck, the bosses. To Glenn Young at Opus Publishing. To D'Arcy Doran for help, advice and encouragement. To Taryn Paterson, a ball-busting bureaucratic high-priestess. All the crazy kids at TCOLondon. To Gabriel Tate, Dan Esam and Lucinda Townend for expert proofreading. To Matt Bochenski, Danny Miller, Paul Willoughby, Rob Longworth and Jonathan Crocker, who started it all. For additional help and access, thanks to Tom Seymour, Kingsley Marshall, Elaine Chow and Mark Salisbury. Thanks to Mario Zucca and all the amazing illustrators. Thanks to Brooklyn's illegal wolf-dog, Vadim Rizov. David Jenkins would like to thank his dear wife Kayte Lawton for putting up with his lack of tidying at the expense of watching obscure subtitled films. Plus Pops and Ma Jenkins, for bankrolling my entire life, and Adam Lee Davis and Paul Fairclough, for lagery spiritual guidance. And Dave Calhoun, for originally letting me write about movies. Sophie Monks Kaufman would like to thank Pieta Monks. Adam Woodward would like to thank Anne and Andrew Woodward, Liz Seabrook, Ian Brookes, Tracey Panayiotou, Sim Eckstein and Will Hitchins. Oliver Stafford would like to thank Cel, Nige and the big brother. Timba Smits would like to thank his fellow team of creative misfits and their ridiculous talent, 'Flash' Gordon Shaw, Vanissa Antonious, Mum and Dad Smits, Summa Grierson, Sarah Hanisch, Ruth Carruthers, Smudge (R.I.P), Sleep (for waiting on me). And Arnold Schwarzenegger.

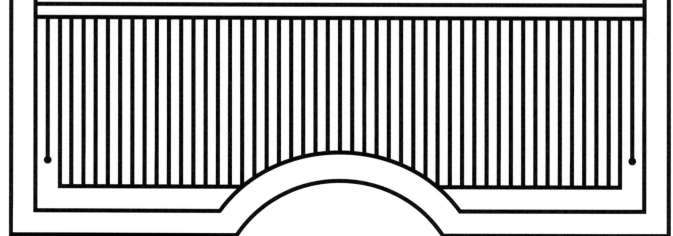